SAM SIXKILLER

SAM SIXKILLER

Cherokee Frontier Lawman

HOWARD KAZANJIAN AND CHRIS ENSS

TWODOT

Guilford, Connecticut
Helena, Montana
An imprint of Globe Pequot Press

A · T W O D O T® · B O O K

Copyright © 2012 by Howard Kazanjian and Chris Enss

Illustration on page 101 by Jeff Galpin

Library of Congress Cataloging-in-Publication Data is available on file.

Kazanjian, Howard.
 Sam Sixkiller : Cherokee frontier lawman / Howard Kazanjian and Chris Enss.
   pages cm
 Includes bibliographical references.
 ISBN 978-0-7627-6075-6
 1. Sixkiller, Sam, 1842–1886. 2. United States marshals—Indian
Territory—Biography. 3. Peace officers—Indian Territory—Biography.
4. Cherokee Indians—Biography. 5. Frontier and pioneer life—Indian
Territory. 6. Indian Territory—Biography. I. Enss, Chris, 1961–
II. Title.
 F697.S59K39 2012
 363.28'2092—dc23
 [B]
                              2012000096

Printed in the United States of America

10 9 8 7 6 5 4 3 2 1

Dedicated to the Native American Lighthorsemen

Contents

FOREWORD

MY AWARENESS OF SAM SIXKILLER GOES BACK TO THE MID-1980S, WHEN
I started in earnest my research on the Indian Territory in present-day
Oklahoma. My interest in the territorial history of the land was primarily focused on Native Americans and African Americans who were outlaws and lawmen. The greatest battleground for law enforcement in the
late nineteenth century was within the Indian and Oklahoma Territories,
which some people called the "Twin Territories." Initially it was just the
Indian Territory; when land was opened up for settlement in 1889, Oklahoma Territory was born. Later, in 1907, both territories would comprise
the state of Oklahoma.

I had never before heard of a famous Native American lawman,
except in the fictional world where we had Tonto, who rode in the shadow
of the Lone Ranger. Sam Sixkiller was the most important Indian lawman that I came across in my research. He was a mixed-blood Cherokee
Indian from the largest tribe in the Indian Territory. The Cherokee origi-
nally were from North Carolina, Tennessee, Kentucky, and Georgia. Their
original homeland was an even larger area of the eastern mountain range
known as the Great Smoky Mountains.

When the British colonized the original colonies, the Cherokee sided with the English monarchy and fought with them during
the French and Indian War. Many Europeans set up shop on Cherokee, Choctaw, Chickasaw, Creek, and Seminole land as traders, trappers, farmers, and soldiers. Those who stayed on Indian land, in many
instances, married Indian women. The offspring of these unions became
known as mixed-bloods.

Mixed-bloods adapted European customs, religions, languages, and agricultural methods. They also became the principal African slave owners in the Indian Nation. With this adaption of European attributes, the Cherokee, Choctaw, Chickasaw, Creek, and Seminole became known by the whites as the Five Civilized Tribes.

Even though the Cherokee adapted to many of the new settlers' customs, their relationship as a whole with the young American nation was rife with conflict. In 1830 President Andrew Jackson wrote and mandated the controversial Indian Removal Act, which was aimed at the Native Americans who lived in the southern portion of the United States. The Cherokee Nation was the largest tribe in the south and was tragically affected by Jackson's edict. The tribe fought removal by appealing to the US Supreme Court, and won its case to stay on its homeland, but Jackson had the military on his side and defied the Supreme Court. What followed became known in Cherokee history as the "Trail of Tears": a massive, forced relocation of Native Americans to the west of the Mississippi River, into an area called the Indian Territory. Tragically, thousands of Indians didn't survive the grueling journey.

The Civil War was bloody and vicious in the Indian Territory; it has not been talked about much and even less has been written about it. The Indian Territory had the highest percentage of loss of life, livestock, and property of any area in the United States during the Civil War. Much of the warfare was guerilla style on both sides, with Stand Watie, the leader of the Cherokee Nation and a brigadier general of the Confederate Army; William Quantrill, a Confederate guerilla leader; Jayhawkers, guerrilla fighters who clashed with pro-slavery advocates from Missouri; Red Legs, a band of militants who refused to join units officially sanctioned by the US Army; and Pin Indians, full-blooded Indians opposed to the South, all fighting and killing each other throughout the territory during the war.

Many of the Indians initially fought with the Confederacy due to their relationship with the slave-holding South and the abandonment of the Indian Territory by the Union Army. Within a year after the start of the Civil War, the Union Army organized three Native American regiments in Kansas known as the Home Guard. These units were critical in the Union's efforts to gain military and political control over the Indian Territory during the war.

Sam Sixkiller joined a Union artillery unit that was commanded by his father, Lieutenant Redbird Sixkiller, who was later a Cherokee judge. The name Sixkiller came from a distant relative who had killed six people in battle many years earlier and became known as Sixkiller, thereby giving this moniker to his descendants, who carried it with distinction.

After the Civil War the Indian Territory became the most dangerous area west of the Mississippi River. There were more US deputy marshals killed in the line of duty in the Indian Nations than anywhere in the United States. The area where the majority of federal peace officers were killed was in the Cherokee Nation.

Besides being a US deputy marshal, Sixkiller was a detective for the Missouri Pacific Railroad and in 1880 became the first captain of the US Indian Police (USIP), which was headquartered at Muskogee, Creek Nation. The USIP served under the Indian agent for the Five Civilized Tribes. Sam Sixkiller came out of this milieu of politics, crime, and upheaval and brought a sense of justice and fairness to the people who lived in the Cherokee Nation and the Indian Territory. Sixkiller became widely known and praised for his law enforcement skills, commitment, and understanding of duty to the job.

It is important that noted storytellers and historians such as Howard Kazanjian and Chris Enss tell this story about one of the most important western frontier lawmen. This book will help illuminate a lawman that stood firm and was dedicated to justice for all. Let's celebrate the legacy of this man and other Indian lawmen that made the American West a special place in US history and culture. I am grateful that Mr. Kazanjian and Ms. Enss decided to take us for this ride of enlightenment in the old Indian Territory, with the redoubtable and magnanimous Cherokee lawman known as Sam Sixkiller.

—Art T. Burton, author/historian

Introduction

ALTHOUGH HIS EXPLOITS ON THE JOB WERE AS COURAGEOUS AS THOSE of Bill Hickok or Wyatt Earp, the name of Sam Sixkiller is scarcely recognized today. The criminal class that invaded the Indian Nation from 1870 to 1886 in the region now known as Oklahoma had to contend with an Indian police force known as the Lighthorsemen, of which Sam Sixkiller was a member. His ability to fearlessly handle horse thieves, bootleggers, murderers, and rapists that perpetrated such illegal acts on Indian land earned him the respect of his people and fellow officers.

As High Sheriff in Tahlequah, the capital of the Cherokee Nation, Sixkiller apprehended white lawbreakers selling rotgut whiskey to Indians and squared off against hostile half-breeds like "Badman" Dick Glass. Glass had a reputation that rivaled Jesse James; some said he was even more ruthless. Sheriff Sixkiller wasn't intimidated by the outlaw and did what was needed to bring him in. Sam Sixkiller not only arrested outlaws and put them in jail but also served as the warden of the very facility that housed the lawbreakers.

From Tahlequah, Sixkiller moved on to Muskogee, in present-day Oklahoma, where he was promoted to captain of the Lighthorsemen and helped to bring peace to the volatile area. When the railroads sliced through the landscape, Captain Sixkiller was named a special agent to the rail lines, thwarting attempted robberies and staving off whiskey peddlers hoping to transport their goods across the territory. Isaac Parker, the famous 12th Judicial Circuit judge who held court at Fort Smith, Arkansas, from 1868 to 1898, was so impressed with Captain Sixkiller's tenacity and dedication to law and order that he recommended the officer be given a commission as a US deputy marshal. These additional responsibilities further exposed the lawman to some of society's most dangerous characters.

A legal altercation between Sixkiller and a pair of violent repeat offenders named Richard Vann and Alf Cunningham sparked a vendetta that eventually led to the lawman's death. Off duty and unarmed, Sixkiller was ambushed and killed by the criminals on Christmas Eve in 1886.

The death of Captain Sixkiller exposed a serious void in federal law as it pertained to those who murdered Native American US deputy marshals: There was nothing on the books that made it a federal offense to kill an Indian officer. Although legislation to correct this deplorable oversight eventually passed, it came too late to affect the cowards that robbed Sixkiller of his life.

Sam Sixkiller died a martyr to the cause of law and order. His story is not only about his life and untimely demise, but also about the everyday life of frontier lawmen and the duties they performed, from the mundane to the perilous.

1

Comes a Lighthorseman

By peace our condition has been improved in the pursuit of civilized life.
—John Ross,
Principal Chief of the Cherokee Nation, 1866

Lawman Sam Sixkiller led his horse through a belt of sparse timber along the Illinois River in southeast Oklahoma Territory. He was a stocky, dark-skinned, heavy-shouldered man with a neatly trimmed, droopy mustache and small dark eyes that were flatly calculating.[1] His eyes shifted purposefully from the streams of sunlight off a growth of blackberry bushes to the rocky path dancing before him. Apart from the sound of his roan's hooves slowly moving through the sweet-gum shrubs and short grass, the only noise was a mingling of a trio of agitated voices wafting through the warm air.[2]

Sam urged his horse into a clearing where three half-blood Cherokee-Seminole Indians sat playing dice.[3] In between rolls of the dice, the men drank from an amber-colored bottle that they eagerly shared with each other. Scattered beside the men were four empty liquor bottles. The drunken Indians barely noticed Sam slowly inching his horse into their crude camp.

The men were undisturbed by Sam's presence and continued with their game. They argued over whose turn it was, nearly coming to blows over which player went next. Sam watched them toss the dice on a thick blanket. At first glance the dusty blanket appeared to be draped over a log.

The closer he got to the action the more it became clear that the make-shift table was actually the body of a fourth Indian. A dark red stream of dried blood had trickled out from under the covering and pooled around a stand of bright orange butterfly weed.

Sam scrutinized the scene more carefully and spotted a massive knife within reach of the Indian closest to him. Sam casually pushed his jacket over the six-shooter strapped on his side, revealing not only the weapon but also the slightly tarnished badge that showed he was a member of the Cherokee Nation police force. One by one the men turned and looked at the lawman. For a breathless instant Sam watched the knife, expecting one of the Indians to snap it up. Without saying a word the three got to their feet, wavering a bit as they did so. Sam pulled his gun out of his holster and leveled it at the men as he eased his five-foot eight-inch frame off his horse. He motioned for the men to back away from the body, and they reluctantly complied. Disgusted, Sam walked over to one of the bottles and kicked it hard. It spun into a nearby rock and broke. What little booze was left inside spilled out and quickly soaked into the dry land.

Sam made his way to the motionless man on the ground and, using the toe of his boot, rolled him over on top of the blanket. The man was dead. There was a deep cut across his throat, and his limbs were stiff.

Possession of liquor on Indian land was a criminal offense. Since being appointed captain of the Indian Police at Union Agency in Muskogee, Creek Nation, in February 1880, Sam had arrested numerous buyers and sellers of liquor. The effect liquor had on many of the men and women in his jurisdiction threatened to destroy the Cherokee way of life. Alcohol had transformed several tribesmen from being proud and self-reliant to careless and irresponsible.[4] Leaders of the Five Civilized Tribes who lived on the reservation that Sam patrolled recognized the ramifications alcoholism had on the people. A Native American elder concerned about the issue lamented, "The Great Spirit, who made all things, made

Captain Samuel Sixkiller 1842–1886. COURTESY OF THE RESEARCH DIVISION OF THE OKLAHOMA HISTORICAL SOCIETY

everything for some use, and whatever use he designed anything for, that use it should be put to. Now, when he made rum, he said, 'Let this be for the Indians to get drunk with.' And it must be so."[5]

Resigned to the consequences of their actions, the men allowed Sam to lead them off to the Muskogee jail in northern Oklahoma Territory. Sam then hauled their dead companion back to his family.

Muskogee, the site of the Indian agency where the heads of the Five Civilized Tribes met, was a sprawling frontier town with a population of more than five hundred people by the early 1800s.[6] The Missouri-Kansas-Texas Railroad (later known as the Missouri Pacific Railroad) stretched across the area, making the town a prime stop for cattlemen wanting to transfer their livestock to buyers on either the east or west coasts.[7] Legitimate businesses, such as hotels, mercantiles, and barbershops, thrived in the busy towns interspersed along the rail line, but criminal activities were abundant as well. Men like Captain Sixkiller were entrusted with suppressing the illegal enterprises, with cattle rustling and bootlegging among the more prevalent crimes. Although the unauthorized production and sale of liquor could be highly profitable, it was a violation of a congressional act. Passed by Congress in the late 1790s, revisions to the Indian Trade and Intercourse Act outlawed the use of liquor in the Indian fur trade. It was later amended to restrict the sale of liquor to Indians under any circumstances.[8]

Government officials, such as Theodore Frelinghuysen, state senator from New Jersey, and Jeremiah Evarts, a Christian missionary and activist for the rights of American Indians, were concerned about preserving the Native American culture. These men believed the Indians' weakness for alcohol made them susceptible to being taken advantage of by white trappers and ambitious land speculators.[9] Along with a number of other political and military leaders, President Andrew Jackson (who held that office from 1829 to 1837) and General Phil Sheridan believed the United States' ultimate goal should be to remove all Indian tribes from the frontier. They held to the idea that liquor used and abused was one of the best ways to ostracize Indians. Gold was the motivating factor behind the president's idea in 1830 and General Sheridan's in 1864. It was also the force behind the westward push of the Cherokee Indians of western North Carolina to eastern Tennessee in 1838.[10]

The Cherokee Indians, who had first occupied and lived peacefully in territories that later became most of Kentucky and Tennessee, were accustomed to being moved off their land. In the late 1820s white settlers pushed the Cherokee to portions of Alabama, Georgia, the Carolinas, Virginia, and West Virginia. From 1684, when the Cherokee Nation established a treaty with English-speaking colonists to retain their native homeland, to the late 1830s, the Cherokee had been forced to relinquish more than 90 percent of their original territory. The domain they held title to in 1838 in the southeastern states had been whittled down to roughly the size of Massachusetts.[11]

By the time gold was discovered on Creek and Cherokee land in southern Georgia in 1828, legislation had already been passed that incorporated the region into the territories of the state. In 1830 President Andrew Jackson authored the Indian Removal Act, which legalized the displacement of entire Indian tribes and paved the way for white prospectors and others to take advantage of the land's rich resources.[12] President Jackson described the Cherokee as "illiterate, uncivilized, savage hunters" and deemed it "in the best interest of everyone to move the Indians out of the territory they occupied." He believed the action would "enable the states to advance rapidly in wealth, population, and power."[13]

Politicians such as Daniel Webster and Henry Clay disagreed with the act proposed by the president and argued against it. They believed the treaties that had been made with the Indians should be honored.[14] After years of debate President Jackson managed to get the signatures needed to get the law passed. The Choctaw Indians in Mississippi were the first to be displaced. In 1836 leaders of the Creek and Cherokee Nations were given two years to get their affairs in order before they were to be escorted to their new home in the region later known as Oklahoma.[15]

But President Jackson underestimated the determination and intelligence of the Cherokee people. With the full backing of his people, Cherokee leader John Ross drafted a petition of protest against the move. The petition was submitted to both Houses of Congress on June 21, 1836; the Houses adjourned on July 4 without ever considering the petition at all.[16] Rumors started circulating that the Indians were on the "war path" and that they planned to massacre non-Indians living in the region. Georgia's Governor William Schley (who held that office from 1835 to 1837) believed the rumors and asked the secretary of war, Lewis Cass, to send

Captain Sixkiller's ancestors, including his parents, were among the Native American people forcibly removed from their homes in the southeast United States to reservations in Oklahoma starting in November 1831. COURTESY OF THE WOOLAROC MUSEUM

in US troops to disarm the Cherokee. More than two thousand federal troops soon arrived on the scene and collected all the Indians' firearms, leaving them nothing they could use for hunting and protection.[17]

Liquor illegally sold and traded to the disillusioned tribes aided the US government in its quest to seize the Indians' property. The consumption of liquor became even more prevalent among the beaten-down tribes. Bootleggers were able to get their product into Indian hands in spite of the laws against it. On the rare occasions when traders could not provide forlorn Indians with liquor, the Indians became resourceful. Some purchased lemon or vanilla extract and used it to become intoxicated. Indians also made their own drinks created from flowers, herbs, and even oak leaves, but none were as potent as drinks made with alcohol.[18]

In 1837 Georgia's Governor George Gilmer (who held that office from 1837 to 1859) ordered the Creek and Cherokee people off their tribal land and had them forcibly relocated to the Oklahoma Territory.[19]

The grueling twenty-two-hundred-mile march across nine states, known as the "Trail of Tears," resulted in the deaths of more than five thousand Indians. They died from disease, starvation, and exposure while en route. The forced relocation left the Creek and Cherokee people broken and dispirited.[20]

Captain Sixkiller presided over a people who resented being driven off their ancestral lands and had an appetite for liquor. In addition to keeping the peace on a reservation filled with fellow Cherokee still struggling to adjust more than fifty years after being displaced, Sam had to contend with animosity between members of the other civilized tribes who lived in the same region.[21] The Seminole Indians, which numbered fewer than any other tribe in the area, believed the domain they were given was less fertile than that of the other tribes.[22] Farming was the only way any of the tribes could sustain themselves. The Seminole Indians complained that their assigned land was hilly, broken, and dense with timber and could not be farmed.[23] The constant threat that all the land given to each of the tribes might be reclaimed by the United States and returned to public land was a source of tension and was considered by some Indians as a justification for criminal behavior.[24]

Captain Sixkiller was part of a law enforcement system that had been established by the Five Civilized Tribes after their move to Oklahoma Territory and was sanctioned by the US government. The duties of the Indian law enforcement agents were to pursue and arrest all perpetrators and fugitives from justice. The May 24, 1881, edition of the *Indian Journal* specifically described the agents' responsibilities as "making arrests for violations of the Intercourse Law by the introduction of liquor; that they had a right to capture and spill liquor; they had a right to arrest any persons in the act of committing felonies or high crimes; they had a right to make fresh pursuit and arrest any person for felonies or high crimes recently after it had been committed; they have the right to maintain order, suppress crowds, arrest rioters, quell disorders, and arrest those who breach the peace. Then above and beyond this power they have a right as citizens to arrest without warrant, to justify such an arrest they must show that a felony or high crime had been committed, and that they had reasonable grounds to believe that the party arrested had been guilty of the crime."[25]

Made up of twenty-six men total, including a captain, lieutenant, and twenty-four horsemen, the group was known as the Lighthorse Company. Indian outlaws arrested by members of the tribal police were tried in court and, if found guilty, punished for their deeds. Repercussions for wrongdoing ranged from execution or imprisonment to social and religious sanctions. Being ostracized from the tribe or not being allowed to participate in ceremonial rituals was considered by many Indians to be a fate worse than jail. Some of the offenses considered to be most serious by the Five Civilized Tribes included murder, rape, and adultery.[26] Prior to the prison being built in Tahlequah, Okla-homa Territory, in 1874, offenders were thrashed with a whip for their crimes. Lighthorsemen used hickory switches to strike the convicted; the lashes numbered twenty-five for misdemeanors and seventy-five for felonies.[27]

For Captain Sixkiller and his cohorts, the day-to-day business of preserving law and order on the reservation did not primarily involve the pursuit of desperados.[28] Rather it consisted of mundane activities like cleaning out irrigation ditches, killing beef cattle for rationing, removing illegal squatters and intruders on Indian land, building roads, transport-ing important messages from one area to another, taking the census, and keeping alcohol at bay.[29]

Liquor presented tribal officials with serious problems. Not only did they have to combat the crimes committed by intoxicated Indians, but they also had to fight against members of the Indian Nation who sold the product to their own people. There was a lot of money to be made selling liquor to the Indians, and opportunistic Native Americans wanted in on the profits. Nefarious Cherokee, Choctaw, Creek, Chickasaw, and Semi-nole Indians stole cattle and horses and traded them for bootleg whiskey.[30] According to a 2009 report of the Bureau of Ethnology, crime escalated substantially in the Oklahoma Territory from the late 1850s through the 1890s because of the bootlegging trade, and Muskogee became the most dangerous town in the territory. During the frontier era more lawmen were killed near Muskogee than anywhere west of the Mississippi River.[31] Sam Sixkiller not only was responsible for keeping order on Indian land during this volatile time, but he also was employed as a US deputy mar-shal and assisted federal posses in the pursuit, capture, and extradition of non-Indian citizens.[32]

Before Sam Sixkiller made his mark in the annals of Indian police history, his father, Redbird "Tor-gu-wha Tah-Tso-Quah" Sixkiller, was interpreting the laws his son would one day uphold. As a chief justice of the Cherokee Supreme Court, Redbird established tribal policies and was responsible for the execution of the law. He was an exceptional student throughout his school years, and, before he graduated, his high marks caught the attention of a Quaker family, who felt he deserved to have his education furthered. The family provided Redbird with the funds to attend school in Newark, Delaware. Enrolled at the Delaware College, he studied law and philosophy.[33]

By 1835 twenty-eight-year-old Redbird had returned to his ancestral home in North Carolina, known as Cherokee Indian Nation East. Efforts to remove Redbird's family, as well as the other Indians in the area, were already under way by the US government. According to an official census taken in December 1835, more than sixteen thousand Cherokee were forced to abandon the territory.[34] Less than a year before the Indians were coerced to leave, Redbird married Pamelia Whaley. Born in March 1810, Pamelia was a half-blood Cherokee. The couple lost their first child, Dewey, on the Trail of Tears. The Sixkillers arrived in the Goingsnake District in the winter of 1837 and settled near the present-day village of Westville, Oklahoma.[35]

With the exception of the thirty-eight hundred members of the Seminole tribe who relocated to the area along with the Sixkillers and other Indians, the people resolved among themselves to make the best of their circumstances. But the Seminole Indians were reluctant to do so. They objected to the US government flooding their land, which had been promised to them in 1832 by President Andrew Jackson, with other Indian tribes. Cherokee leaders, such as Chief John Ross and later Redbird Sixkiller, acted as mediators to arrest the hostility between the Seminole Indians and the United States.[36] Their efforts were recognized by the House of Representatives in the spring of 1838. Congressman Henry A. Wise from Virginia told politicians, "The Cherokee mediators went at the risk of their own lives and penetrated within the lines of the bitter Seminole forces. They discharged their mission with satisfaction and integrity. We owe them our thanks."[37]

Redbird's assistance helped bring some peace to the explosive region. Fueled by the example of his father's unwavering determination to uphold justice, as well as his deep faith in his own people, Sam was charged with carrying on that duty.

2

Principals of Peace

Circumstances that cannot be controlled, and which are beyond the reach of human laws, render it impossible that you can flourish in the midst of a civilized community. You have but one remedy within your reach. And that is, to remove to the West and join your countrymen, who are already established.

—President Andrew Jackson
to the Cherokee Tribe of Indians, April 7, 1835

The sweeping prairie lay quietly under the heat of a brassy sun as a lone wagon topped a grassy knoll that afforded an arresting view from every direction. Redbird Sixkiller drove the team of two horses pulling the wagon toward the town of Tahlequah, Oklahoma Territory, in the near distance. His four-year-old son, Sam, sat beside him captivated by the sights and listening intently to the stories Redbird told about his ancestors and the origin of the Sixkiller family name. Redbird shared with Sam a tale about one of their fearless relatives. The ancestor was engaged in battle against the Creek Indians and had killed six braves and then himself before another band of hostile Creek Indians that surrounded him could attack. The Cherokee Indian warriors who witnessed the daring act referred to the warrior as Sixkiller.[1]

Given the courageous example Sixkiller had set, Redbird felt he owed it to the legendary Cherokee to face with the same fortitude the trials that lay ahead for the Indian Nation. It was a pathetic group of thousands of Indians who were herded west during the winter of 1838–39. Redbird Sixkiller's recollection of the grueling journey that came to be known as the Trail of Tears was passed along to his son, his son's sons, and every generation that followed. The January 18, 1972, edition of the Statesville, North Carolina, newspaper, the *Statesville Daily Record,* published Redbird's reminiscences as told by those generations and noted that the inhumanity of the forced move of the Indians preyed on his sense of justice. He saw helpless Cherokee arrested, dragged from their homes, and driven at bayonet point into the stockades. He watched as his people were loaded like cattle into wagons and hauled west. Redbird told Sam how few of the Indians were given time to make arrangements to leave and that one family was driven from its home as members were preparing to bury a child who had died. He recounted how another mother forced from her home fell and died of a heart attack before they could take her to the stockade. Still another mother died of pneumonia contracted after giving her only blanket for the protection of a sick child.[2]

Sam listened intently to his father describe a Cherokee elder's reaction to the tragic event. The elder's name was Chief Junaluska. During the Battle of the Horse Shoe, the chief saved the life of a man who would eventually become the president of the United States, and who would support the relocation of Indian tribes. The chief later admitted that if he had known the life he was saving was that of Andrew Jackson, American history would have been written differently.[3]

Like many other Indians who survived the Trail of Tears, Redbird passed on to his son the stories of how government soldiers treated the Cherokee during this time. Only a few men were remembered for being humane. The majority of officers and the members of their units treated the Indians harshly. A soldier with the Georgia volunteers who showed sympathy to the Cherokee described in his memoirs the severity of the treatment the Indians received. "I fought through the War Between the

States," the veteran recounted, "and I have seen men shot to pieces by the thousands, but the Cherokee removal was the cruelest work I ever knew."[4]

Redbird also passed along the story of how he met Sam's mother during the ordeal. Their first meeting occurred a few days prior to embarking on the trip to the Indian Territory. Redbird recalled how he and Pamelia sat with clasped hands gazing out across the valley, realizing that the smoke of dying fires in the little homes soon to be abandoned would someday be only a painful memory. They knew that within a few days they would have to say farewell to each other and all they knew. At dawn the bugle would blow and the wagon train would begin to wind its weary way through the low-timbered hills on an unmarked trail, leading them all to an unknown region to begin a new life among the wild tribes of the West.[5]

On the last day they stood side by side as the sun disappeared. No tears were shed, no words were spoken—the moment was too sacred for mere words. A quick embrace, a whispered good-bye was all they shared. She mounted her little pony, Smokey, and galloped away into the gathering dusk, while he stalked stoically up the hill with the dying echo of Smokey's hoofbeats in his ears.[6]

Redbird believed he would never be happy again. On the evening of the third day, the caravan halted for the night. The smoke of many campfires could be seen far ahead, as Redbird's people prepared for the evening meals, cared for the sick and weary children, and comforted the old folks uprooted from their homes and fearful of the new lands ahead. Redbird squatted before the fire, gazing into the dying ashes and listening to the familiar noises of the descending night. His mind was not upon the end of the trail but back along the way he had traveled and to his lovely Pamelia.[7]

Suddenly his old saddle horse, which was hitched behind the wagon, raised its head and nickered. Redbird caught the faint thud of hoofs in the valley below the camp drawing nearer, awakening a familiar echo in his mind of the little feet of Smokey. He watched a cloud of dust drawing near, noting the well-known outlines of the little pony, and with a glad cry rushed to where Smokey had halted just within the circle of the light cast by the campfire. He reached up, and Pamelia fell nearly unconscious into his arms and faintly whispered, "Redbird."[8]

Conversation between father and son died down as they rode into Tahlequah. Thousands of Cherokee Indians from the eastern and western portions of the state had descended upon the location to attend a convention that promised to unite the two factions. Since being removed from their native homes, divided, and sent to live at opposite ends of the territory, the Cherokee people had been battling among themselves.[9] The central theme of the convention was "one body politic under the style and title of the Cherokee Nation."[10] Redbird and Sam attended the ambitious eleven-day meeting in August 1846 along with more than two thousand other Indians.[11] Redbird wanted his son to see the efforts being made to resolve the violent conflict that had erupted between the groups.

The factions did not agree on the concessions that should be made to the US government over their native land. The Cherokee in the east, led by the Principal Chief of the Cherokee Indians from 1828 to 1867, were opposed to leaving their homeland no matter what the government had promised in exchange. Those in the west, led by Cherokee National Council member John Ridge, were in favor of the removal of the Cherokee to the region later known as Oklahoma Territory, as well as full acceptance of the funds and improved provisions that accompanied the move.[12] Specifically, the US government had offered the Cherokee people twenty million dollars in annuities for land cession to be held in a trust and paid out to each individual of the nation, along with a guarantee that the land they occupied in the Oklahoma region would be regarded as solely their land for the common use and benefit of all Cherokee.[13]

The eastern Cherokee faction did not trust the federal government to honor any agreement made. John Ross had tried to negotiate with the

United States in 1835 and persuade it to leave his people with some of their native land. But nothing short of complete removal of the Indians would do. John Ridge, representing the Cherokees from the west, believed there was no choice for the Indian but to settle with the government and accept its word that the government would deliver what it promised.[14]

Redbird was in favor of the Cherokee people coming together as one. He felt that the prosperity and welfare of the Cherokee Nation, and of his family, depended upon an undivided front. He agreed with the treaty drafted by Washington politicians in July 1846 and quoted a portion of the preamble to Sam, which read: "Whereas serious difficulties have, for a considerable time past, existed between the different portions of the people constituting and recognized as the Cherokee Nation of Indians, which it is desirable should be speedily settled, so that peace and harmony may be restored among them. . . ."[15]

Many US politicians, including President James K. Polk, doubted that the two groups could ever peacefully coexist. President Polk told his staff, "I am satisfied that there is no probability that the different parties into which (the Cherokee Nation) is divided can ever again live together in harmony."[16] John Ridge disagreed and responded by saying, "Cherokee blood, if not destroyed, will win its course in beings of fair complexions, who will read that their ancestors became civilized under the frowns of misfortune, and the causes of their enemies."[17] For the sake of his son Sam, his one-year-old daughter, and his children yet to be born, Redbird had to believe the Cherokee Nation would band together.

In spite of the pessimists, the factions were able to set aside their differences and establish a basis of government by which all Cherokee could live. Sam witnessed firsthand Indian leaders setting up their own government, one that was similar to that of the United States. Three branches were established: the executive, which consisted of a chief assistant and six executive councilors; the legislative, a forty-member committee that met once a year; and the judiciary, in which Redbird would later serve.[18]

Redbird hoped reunification of the Cherokee people and the organization of a legitimate government would lead to a decrease in the increasingly prevalent Indian-against-Indian crimes of horse theft, robbery, and murder. Try as they might, the Cherokee Nation's mounted police, the Lighthorsemen, were unable to stop the illegal activities completely. Some Indians felt the Lighthorsemen only arrested and punished the Cherokee Indians who had been against the move to the Oklahoma Territory. Men and women who believed the police were biased often retaliated against them.

One particularly incendiary altercation involved the killing of James Starr and Suel Rider. Starr and Rider, both former members of the National Cherokee Committee who favored relocation, were murdered by rogue members of the police.[19] When the Lighthorsemen finally caught up with the lawmen who were out to kill any Indian leader who had signed the agreement to leave their native Cherokee land, they were shot and killed on the spot. Anonymous letters sent to the newspaper the *Cherokee Advocate* on November 11, 1845, insisted that Indian outlaws who had willingly agreed to sign a treaty with the United States in exchange for their land were never treated as harshly for their misdeeds.[20] White Indian agents aware of the controversy were sent in by the government to intercede.

On November 15, 1846, the government ordered the acting chief of the Cherokee, George Lowrey, to consider doing away with the Lighthorsemen to avoid further problems. Chief Lowrey not only refused but also expressed his displeasure with the government's interference. In a letter to Cherokee agent Colonel James McKisick on November 26, 1846, the chief reminded the colonel that the subject of the Lighthorsemen, crime, and the US government's influence over the Indians had been thoroughly discussed at the Tahlequah convention. He further added that the charges against the Lighthorsemen were unfounded. "There is but one company in the Nation—for all the Nation. With but two exceptions, Lighthorsemen have committed no murder. . . . There is sufficient moral virtue among the Cherokee to recover from these disturbances, if left to the free exercise of their prerogatives."[21]

"All matters were of great importance," Redbird told Sam several years after attending the convention. "Without an alliance among our people the tribe would not have survived."[22] With great hope that a peaceful future was on the horizon, Redbird and Sam returned to Westville after the conference and went straight to work growing their farm.

By 1861 the Sixkiller homestead included a large, two-story log house, several acres of corn and wheat, three hundred hogs, and one hundred head of cattle.[23] After losing their firstborn before settling in Oklahoma Territory, Redbird and Pamelia had another eight children. Sam, who was born on November 25, 1842, was educated with his three sisters and four brothers at a nearby Baptist mission.[24] According to the December 29, 1886, edition of the *Indian Journal* newspaper, in an article written after Sam's death, Sam and his siblings were good students.[25] Sam strived to keep his school marks high to make his father as proud of him as he was of his father.

As a young boy Sam idolized his father. Redbird patiently taught Sam and his brothers how to hunt and work the land. A variety of wild game, including deer and turkey, roamed the Sixkiller homestead. Redbird also made sure his family assisted those in the area who needed help with their farms. The Sixkillers, along with many other Indians, came to the aid of tribesmen who needed their land cleared and timber cut.[26] Redbird taught his children the importance of generosity and tradition. He shared a portion of the family's crops and game with other members of the Cherokee Nation at ceremonial dances and feasts.

The Stomp Dance was one of the most popular events the Sixkillers attended. The name of the dance refers to the shuffle and stomp movements involved. Held where the tribe got its water, the dance lasted several days, and people would come from many parts of the country to participate.

In addition to Redbird's work ethic and commitment to the importance of tribal ritual, Sam admired how well respected his father was among the Indian leaders. He watched him struggle with the other tribes to control the influx of white criminals to their area. US law enforcement officials could not follow whites across the borders of the Indian Territory, making Oklahoma Territory a safe retreat for white lawbreakers.[27] Desperados frequently snuck through the Sixkiller's farmland, helping themselves to whatever supplies they needed. Redbird ran intruders off his property, but to no avail.[28] The number of trespassers continually increased and, short of gunning them all down, little could be done.

In 1861 Redbird's attention, along with that of the other members of the Five Civilized Tribes living in the Oklahoma area, shifted from protecting their territory to protecting the Union. The Civil War divided the people of the United States and brought more turmoil to the Cherokee people. The two factions of the Indian Nation disagreed on whether to support the Confederacy or the Union. The more affluent members of the two groups sided with the southern states. As several wealthy Cherokee Indians owned slaves, they agreed with the South's position on slavery and property. Affluent white people from Southern states who made their home in the Cherokee Nation in the 1800s brought with them property they owned (including slaves), as well as their own unique customs. When they married Cherokee Indians, their goods and traditions followed them and were passed on from generation to generation. Less than 3 percent of Cherokee Indians owned slaves. Cherokee who were traditionalists were anti-slavery and favored the Union during the Civil War.[29]

Redbird joined the Union army on July 11, 1861. After his training he was commissioned as a first lieutenant in the Union Artillery of the Second Brigade. He fought at the Battle of Newtonia in Missouri in September 1862. The battle was the first during the Civil War in which Indians played a significant part on both sides. Redbird went on to fight battles in Arkansas at Cane Hill and Prairie Grove.[30]

When Redbird enlisted in the military, he left nineteen-year-old Sam in charge of the farm. Like other young men who stayed behind to care for the homestead, Sam worked hard to keep things in order.[31] Because the war created shortages of various foods and supplies in the area, Sam's brother Luke's wife, Emma, recalled in her memoirs that they drank coffee made from "wheat bran or roasted corn. . . . Our tea was spice bush wood sweetened with molasses made from pumpkins," she elaborated. "Bread was $10 and couldn't be got very often. Our clothing was very scant and wild game hard to come by. . . . The children cried from being hungry."[32]

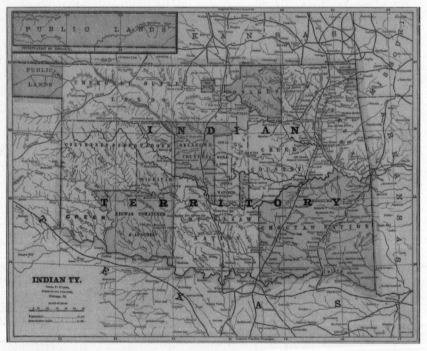

Indian Territory Map—1888. This map shows the area to which the Five Civilized Tribes were assigned by the federal government. Captain Sixkiller traveled throughout the region in search of outlaws. COURTESY OF THE RESEARCH DIVISION OF THE OKLAHOMA HISTORICAL SOCIETY

Soldiers from both sides invaded the area from time to time. Control was passed from South to North and back again. Plow horses were taken from the Sixkiller farm. Livestock was driven off or shot. Furniture and personal belongings were confiscated by rogue troops, and some Indians were thrown out of their homes into the cold. "Mothers sat up all night to keep fires burning and themselves and their children from freezing," Emma Sixkiller shared in her memoirs.[33] Sam's friends and neighbors resented the treatment and abandoned their homes to join in the fight. They encouraged Sam to come along with them. He resisted at first but eventually changed his mind.

On May 1, 1862, Sam joined the rebel forces. He served as a Confederate soldier for less than a year, and he never engaged in any fighting. The thought that he might face his father on the field of battle led him to reconsider the side he was on. By spring 1863 Sam had left his unit with the Confederacy and joined the Union Army.[34]

Sam traveled from the Arkansas-Georgia area to Fort Gibson, Oklahoma Territory. There he signed a three-year contract to fight for the North. Sam was assigned to Company L, an infantry troop made up of Indian guards originating out of Kansas. Redbird was stationed at the same Midwest location and was the officer in charge of Company L.[35] Father and son helped prepare and defend the fort and surrounding acreage from rebel Indian soldiers like Stand Watie, commander of the Indian cavalry. Watie led more than eight hundred Cherokee, Seminole, and Creek soldiers in an attack against Union troops north of Fort Gibson, which resulted in the capture of a Union steamer ship and the death of numerous troops.[36]

During Sam's absence, his mother, brothers, and sisters endured several raids by guerrilla white soldiers known as bushwhackers. The bushwhackers preyed on defenseless individuals and families in rural areas, stealing crops and cattle. On the evening of July 30, 1863, bushwhackers overtook the Sixkiller farm, setting fire to the stable and the barn. Pamelia

Sixkiller was fatally shot trying to protect her children. The infant son she held tightly in her arms was also killed.[37] Before she died, she asked her eighteen-year-old daughter, Mary, to take care of the other children. Pamelia and her nineteen-month-old son, William, were buried at the Baptist Mission Cemetery in Adair, Oklahoma.[38] Redbird finally returned home in May 1865.

Sam also was mustered out of the service in May 1865. After paying $0.40 to the military for "equipage lost" and collecting his final wages totaling $9.18, he returned to Westville.[39] The Oklahoma Territory that the Cherokee Nation occupied had been ravaged by the war. Farms and businesses were leveled, fields lay in ruin, and what little livestock remaining were feeble and sick. More than a third of the Cherokee population died during the Civil War. Tribe members who survived the ordeal gathered in small groups and combed the land looking for food.[40]

Indians who fled the area when the war erupted slowly began to return to the Oklahoma Territory, but the problems that existed prior to the conflict between the states escalated as the Cherokee rebuilt their homes and settlements, and the tribe split into factions again. According to an August 1865 report from Secretary of Interior James Harlan, Indian agents were being inundated with complaints that not enough was being done by the US government to uphold the law.[41] The tribal police force—the Lighthorsemen—was not operating at full capacity any longer, as most of the lawmen had joined the fight between the states and were not available to patrol the territory. Due to the absence of any other law enforcement agency, deserters from the military, thieves, unscrupulous land barons, and bootleggers were allowed to commit crimes on Cherokee property, flee to other regions, and return unpunished.[42]

Oklahoma was not yet part of the Union; it was merely a territory. US officials like Senator James Doolittle of Wisconsin explained to Indian leaders that with no state or federal lawmen to intercede, the tribe had to police the area the best it could. Redbird helped organize the Citizen's

Court and the Executive Council of the Goingsnake District to deal with the strife among the Cherokee people. The Citizen's Court and the Executive Council heard arguments, settled disputes, and determined policies. Redbird was later elected judge of the council and assisted in reestablishing the Lighthorse Company.[43]

Sam supported his father's work on behalf of the Cherokee people but initially had no interest in politics. His focus was on restoring the family farm and spending time with Frances "Fannie" Forman, the Sixkillers' neighbor's nineteen-year-old daughter. Fannie and Sam were married in September 1865 and moved to Tahlequah, the capital of the Cherokee Nation. According to the 1896 edition of the *Tahlequah City Directory*, the capital was situated "amid a quartet of wooded hills, from whose base flows numerous health-giving springs of pure water, and is surrounded by some of the finest farming land in the world. Wood, water, and grass are in abundance."[44] Sam worked his own homestead in the fertile valley. On May 5, 1870, he and Fannie had twin girls, Rachel and Eliza. Minnie was born in 1871. Two years later the couple had a fourth daughter, who they named Emma. On September 4, 1874, Fannie gave birth to a fifth daughter named Cora.[45]

Redbird was proud of Sam's accomplishments but wanted him to consider pursuing a career in law enforcement. He was aware of the growing need for Indian police. In 1866 Redbird was appointed to a committee to negotiate an agreement with the Union Pacific Railroad for construction of a railroad through Cherokee land. Redbird suspected that some Indians would be opposed to the railroad and that there might be an increase in crime as a result of the railway.[46] Tracklayers and graters looking to steal a payroll shipment and robbers lying in wait to hijack the trains were foremost among his concerns. Redbird also anticipated more white settlers encroaching on the Cherokee Nation because of the railroad, which would lead to further unrest for the tribe. Competent, fearless policemen were necessary to maintain peace. Sam exhibited

A06

Redbird Sixkiller: Soldier, judge, and prominent leader of the Cherokee Nation.

independence and strength, which convinced Redbird that Sam was qualified for the job.

Sam eventually succumbed to his father's urgings and in 1874 agreed to be appointed as High Sheriff of Tahlequah. Each district in the Cherokee Nation had its own sheriff—the equivalent of the sheriff of a county in the states—and the High Sheriff was the head of all the district officers. The same year Sam took office, the Cherokee National Prison was built. The large, sandstone rock structure was built for the purpose of rehabilitation as well as punishment of offenders. It was three stories high and housed both sentenced and accused prisoners from throughout the vast territory. Accounts at the time noted it was "made to hold the most hardened and dangerous prisoners."[47] Sam's job was to carry out the sentences of the Cherokee courts, which were moving away from corporal punishment to a policy of detention. When ordered, he also carried out death sentences. It was said that "no one escaped unless through death; some condemned prisoners were hanged on a scaffold behind the prison in the courtyard."[48]

Sam earned five hundred dollars a year for his services, which included working as the treasurer and custodian of the facility. On acreage adjacent to the prison, he used his talent for farming to grow corn for the inmates and hay and grain for the livestock.[49] The prisoners were required to work in the farm or at the national brickyard.[50] Bricks from the yard were used to construct several new buildings in the Tahlequah town square.

Like his father, Sam was well respected. He was a conscientious lawman who did not tolerate disorderly conduct. He enjoyed his work and planned to make the capital his permanent home, purchasing several lots in the heart of the city for himself, his wife, and their growing family.[51]

Not everyone appreciated the dedication to duty that Sam possessed or the idea that he would be staying on in Tahlequah. Criminals like Cherokee half-blood Dick Vann, who preyed on residents of the

Cherokee Nation, resented any attempt to bring about law and order. Vann and other outlaws like him saw Sam as the primary stumbling block in their quest to make a living stealing livestock, operating houses of ill fame, and selling alcohol to Indians.[52] In the late 1870s bootleg whiskey sold for four dollars a gallon, and thousands of gallons were flowing into the Indian Nation.[53] Backed by orders from the Indian agents, Sam promised to apprehend anyone involved in nefarious ventures, thus becoming the target for many of the most dangerous characters in the region.

3

Trouble in Tahlequah

Surely it is hard sometimes to find consolation in the words "God's will be done."

—Reporter for the *Cherokee Advocate*
about the shooting death of a
rowdy Tahlequah citizen, November 30, 1878

Willis Pettit, a tall, well-built black man, sank his spurs into his horse's back end and the animal, already moving at a fast pace, quickened its stride. The anxious rider chanced a glance over his shoulder to see if he was being followed. In the rapidly disappearing landscape there was no sign of any other rider. A flash of relief passed over his face.

Sheriff Sam Sixkiller, who was in pursuit of Pettit and had anticipated the route the fleeing criminal would take, waited for him at a ford in the Illinois River several miles outside of Tahlequah. The sheriff's horse carried him over the rocks through a shallow section of water, then dropped its head to the surface and eagerly drank. Sam swung himself crossways in the saddle, lifted the canteen hanging off the horn, opened the container, and took a long swig. He carefully scanned the scenery around him as he hopped off his horse and plunged his canteen into the water to refill it. The sound of a fast-approaching horse made him pause for a moment. The sheriff returned the canteen to his saddle, then lifted his rifle out of its holster. Turning slowly toward the sound, he leveled his gun in the direction of the oncoming steed.

Pettit and his ride emerged from the thicket that flanked the river on both sides and followed the incline to the water's edge. The horse spooked and reared back when it came upon Sheriff Sixkiller, and Pettit was thrown to the ground. Before he could even get to his feet, he was staring down the barrel of the sheriff's gun. He raised his hands in surrender, cursing his luck in the process.[1]

On May 15, 1876, Sheriff Sixkiller arrested Willis Pettit for "assault with intent to kill Emanuel Spencer with a pistol."[2] It was the first of many arrests for Pettit in the Cherokee Nation during Sam's time in office. Pettit, a former slave, aligned himself with other ex-slaves who believed they were entitled to a section of the territory that had been given to the Five Civilized Tribes. They argued that, as restitution, slaves owned by the Cherokee, Chickasaw, Choctaw, Creek, and Seminole tribes who were freed after the Civil War should be granted a part of the region for their own exclusive use. With the exception of the Seminole Indians, every tribe disagreed with the idea, and the conflict sparked controversy and, at times, violence.[3]

The post-Civil War government agreed that slaves once owned by Indians were full citizens of their nation with equal rights in annuities and land allotments. In 1866 the federal government drafted new treaties with the Five Civilized Tribes and incorporated the rights of the former slaves, known as tribal Freedmen, into those treaties. Cherokee leaders argued against land ownership for tribal Freedmen. As a result early attempts by the Freedmen to build homes and businesses in the Indian Nation were not successful. Some Indians set fire to the structures and attempted to drive the emancipated men and women out of the region. The tribal Freedmen refused to go. The idea of trying to build a life among whites that opposed the outcome of the Civil War was considered far more risky. The Freedmen eventually were allowed to work and farm their

Sheriff Sixkiller crisscrossed this riverbed many times in pursuit of outlaws.
COURTESY OF THE RESEARCH DIVISION OF THE OKLAHOMA HISTORICAL SOCIETY

plots of land in peace, and for most that was sufficient.[4] But for others, like Willis Pettit, it was not enough.

Sheriff Sixkiller deposited Pettit at the National Prison, where more than fifteen other inmates were being housed. The bulk of the captives had begun their stay at the prison seven months prior to Pettit's arrest. The local newspaper described the arrival of ten offenders on November 25, 1876. "A wagon filled with people proceeded by a pair of well-dressed men who looked like officers paraded into the area.... Half the town was soon at the heels of the party, curious to see the operation of imprisonment practically illustrated. Standing at our window, we could see the prisoners handed over one by one, to disappear behind the stone walls and front doors, which had been erected such [sic] from abusing their liberty. We could not help thinking what folly must have possessed them our favored country—favored beyond any on earth in respect of natural vantages—to violate laws so easy to observe."[5]

Sheriff Sixkiller's position with the Indian Nation went well beyond rresting and holding men like Willis Pettit accountable for breaking the law. The structure Sheriff Sixkiller oversaw was built in 1874 for six thousand dollars. Those who participated in the construction of the prison facility and the gallows claimed that "no one escaped unless through death; condemned prisoners were taken to be hanged on a scaffold behind the courtyard." The Cherokee National Prison was created for reformation as well as punishment of offenders. According to the law, "punishment could include hard labor, solitary confinement, or imprisonment and confinement therein at hard labor." It was used "when deemed expedient for the safe keeping of persons charged with murder, or other high crimes, and the temporary confinement or punishment of persons sentenced by the National Council or who may be put under arrest for drunkenness, or other misdemeanors at the seat of government. The Principal Chief had the power to pardon condemned men, with the advice and consent of the Executive Council, but this was rarely exercised." The prison was the only such facility in the entire Indian Nation from 1875[6] to 1901.

Sheriff Sixkiller acted as warden, treasurer, and chief custodian. His responsibilities included contracting for supplies and labor in and for the prison; settling all bills; superintending the police of the prison; securing some minister of the Gospel to hold divine service in the prison, instructing prisoners in their moral and religious duties and visiting the sick among them; providing discharged convicts with a decent suit of clothes not to exceed five dollars in value; preserving all money and effects in the possession of convicts; requiring all subordinates to refrain from the use of boisterous, harsh, and unbecoming language to the prisoners and to each other while in and about the prison; and maintaining a list of convicts received, discharged, and pardoned, as well as who died during the year.[7]

The sheriff's job was nearly impossible to do with the limited help he had, so when he decided to upgrade the facility in the early spring of 1877, he used prisoners to do the labor. Pettit was in and out of the jail during this time and assisted with the various improvements. According to the April 11, 1877, edition of the *Cherokee Advocate,* "Sheriff Sixkiller . . . is having a wall put around the National Prison—solid boards, ten feet high, which enclosed two acres of ground, and adds to the look and safety of the institution muchly."[8]

Tahlequah residents were in favor of using convicts to do the labor and applauded Sheriff Sixkiller's resourcefulness. "They work as well, if not better than those who are footloose," the *Cherokee Advocate* observed.

Cherokee National Prison at Tahlequah, taken August 1967. COURTESY OF THE RESEARCH DIVISION OF THE OKLAHOMA HISTORICAL SOCIETY

"They want to profit by their confinement they say, and had rather work than be idle." The inmates were hired out at one dollar a day in National Prison tickets.[9] These tickets could be used to purchase items at the prison store, such as tobacco, canned food, and soap.

In addition to maintaining the prison and improving the property, Sheriff Sixkiller introduced rehabilitation programs to the prisoners. Shoemaking, blacksmithing, and wagon-making shops were organized, and inmates were taught the various trades. As one of the directors of the Tahlequah school, Sheriff Sixkiller also made arrangements for teachers and books to be available to help illiterate inmates learn to read and write.[10] The inspiration Sheriff Sixkiller had for reformation within the prison came from a directive issued by the Prison Commission established in 1876 in England, which was adopted in the United States in 1877. He agreed with the shift in the treatment of prisoners from harsh and brutal confinement to a more humane and productive means of discipline.[11]

To assist in his duties of rounding up lawbreakers like Pettit along with a growing number of bootleggers, Sheriff Sixkiller recruited several trustworthy and capable deputies. Among the members on his staff were his younger brothers Luke and Martin.[12] Later his administration would benefit from the expertise of lawman Charles LeFlore. LeFlore played a key role in the pursuit of the outlaws Butch Cassidy and the Sundance Kid.[13]

Sheriff Sixkiller's law enforcement team was on hand during a violent incident that took place on a cold afternoon in mid-November 1878. A frigid breeze blew through Tahlequah's Capital Square, and people coming in and out of the various shops and crossing the main thoroughfare pulled their coats close and shielded their eyes from the icy wind. Sheriff Sixkiller scanned the street from his office inside the prison. Somewhere in the distance he heard galloping horses and a volley of shots.[14]

Suddenly a handful of young Cherokee riders charged into town, whooping and hollering, their guns blazing. They chased the frightened townspeople, who scattered in all directions. Some terrified people dove into doors of nearby businesses, seeking cover from rogue bullets and stampeding hooves. The sheriff hurried out of his office and joined the other policemen attempting to stop the wild bucks. Sheriff Sixkiller shouted for the men to halt, but they wouldn't listen. He took aim at the men and fired a couple of times. One of his shots nicked a fleeing horse in one of its legs. The horse faltered a bit, and the Indian riding the animal struggled to stay on its back.[15]

According to eyewitnesses, the horses carried the rioters out of town at full gallop. The sheriff and his deputies chased after them. One of the men, Jeter Thompson, turned in his saddle and fired at Sam. A hail of bullets whipped past the lawman's head. The other riders followed suit. The sheriff was furious and called for his deputies to open fire. The sheriff and Deputy Cullos Thorne fired bullets that hit Thompson in the stomach, and he fell off his horse. His friends didn't stop but rode quickly out of town.[16]

Deputies and concerned citizens hurried over to Thompson's bleeding body. He was writhing in pain when Sheriff Sixkiller arrived at the spot where Thompson had fallen from his horse. The young man resisted any attempt to stem the flow of blood pouring out of his midsection. He searched the faces around him looking for the sheriff's. Wincing, he accused the sheriff of having a grudge against him. "That's why you shot me," he told him.[17] Thompson was transported to the local doctor's office where he died on November 23, 1878. According to the newspaper, the *Indian Journal,* dated December 5, 1878, "Thompson died not only of complications from gunshot wounds but complications from pneumonia."[18]

Thompson's friends and family were at his bedside when he passed. When Thompson wasn't participating in ride-by shootings, he was a junior member of the mercantile business known as J. Thompson and Son. His parents, brothers, sisters, and wife remembered him as a "worthy member of the mercantile circle, a dutiful son, beloved brother, and affectionate husband." Thompson left behind an estate worth more than three thousand dollars.[19]

Jeter Thompson's family was furious with what they viewed as overzealous actions by the town's law enforcement officials. The slain man's parents believed the sheriff had abused the power of his office. They admitted the rowdy riders were acting irresponsibly but insisted they had no intention of hurting anyone.[20] Thompson's parents wanted the accusation their son made on his deathbed investigated and demanded the sheriff vacate his position until the incident was thoroughly reviewed. J. F. Thompson, the Principal Chief, Executive Secretary of the Cherokee Nation (no direct relation to the shooting victim), and George Downing Johnson, Executive Councilor of the Goingsnake District, agreed.[21] Sheriff Sixkiller refused to step down. Regardless of an investigation or its outcome, the sheriff maintained he had properly defended himself and the people of Tahlequah.[22]

Bootleggers who thought they could take advantage of the problems the sheriff and his administration were experiencing found out the lawman wasn't distracted from upholding the law. On June 4, 1879, the sheriff and his men arrested a white man named Solomon Coon for bringing ten gallons of whiskey into the Cherokee Nation to sell to the Indians. Solomon transported the liquor in five-gallon barrels affixed to the back of a wagon. He was fined $750 and placed in jail for an undisclosed amount of time. It wouldn't be the last time Solomon would be arrested for bootlegging.[23]

Three days after Solomon was apprehended, the Cherokee leaders looking into the shooting death of Jeter Thompson concluded that the sheriff and three of his deputies should be charged with murder and

malpractice of office. George Downing Johnson sent a letter inform-
ing Principal Chief Thompson about the charges and requesting that
he "appoint someone to take over Sixkiller's position until the mitiga-
tion and trial is over because it might be used for the advantage of the
accused."[24]

The June 11, 1879, edition of the Tahlequah *Cherokee Advocate* newspaper announced that Sam Sixkiller, Cullos Thorne, Richard Robinson,
and John Boston had been arrested "upon a preliminary warrant sworn
out before the Clerk by the Solicitor of this district. . . . The preliminary examination will be held on Thursday the 12th."[25] Principal Chief
Thompson (whose term in office was close to an end) appointed Samuel
Downing as temporary High Sheriff. Captain Sixkiller was livid and
objected to turning over control of his job to Downing. Sixkiller informed
his replacement that Downing would have to forcibly remove him from
the premises to take over the position. Downing let the Principal Chief
know where Sheriff Sixkiller stood and quickly sent another letter warning the stubborn lawman to acquiesce. Principal Chief Thompson set
a deadline of July 2, 1879, for Sheriff Sixkiller to turn over the books,
papers, and records of the National Prison. He warned Sixkiller that if he
failed to comply there would be serious consequences. The sheriff reluctantly obeyed the order.[26]

The investigation was much more encompassing than Sheriff
Sixkiller had anticipated. Suspicion about on-the-job misconduct spread
to his running of the National Prison. On July 22, 1879, a special committee of the Indian Council was appointed to investigate the affairs of
the prison.[27]

Sheriff Sixkiller then retained two attorneys from the law firm
Detense, Boudinot, Rasmus, Walker, and Johnson to "attend to any and
all business connected in any way with the office of High Sheriff and the
National Prison during the last few years ending in November 1879."[28]

The difficulties Sheriff Sixkiller was experiencing went beyond the confines of his office. His home life was suffering a great deal as a result of the controversy that now surrounded him. Not only were he and his wife, Fannie, not getting along, but she had also contracted consumption. Her condition was exacerbated by the stress of worrying about what would happen to her husband and how they would provide for their family if he lost his job. There was also news that the sheriff was having an affair. The gossip that reached Fannie included talk that the lawman had fathered children with his alleged mistress.[29]

Sheriff Sixkiller defended himself against the notion that he had been less than faithful to Fannie and assured her that he would find work outside of law enforcement. He promised that he would never leave her, particularly in a time of crisis. Fannie promised the same.

Opening statements at Sam Sixkiller's trial and that of three of his deputy/guards were heard on June 18, 1879. The lawman's attorneys told members of the jury that on the day of Jeter Thompson's unfortunate demise, their clients were performing their duties as they were sworn to do and had been fired on first. According to the defendants, Thompson and his friends had charged recklessly through the town on other occasions prior to the November 1878 incident. Each time the young men rode into Tahlequah firing their weapons and frightening townspeople. They had been warned to stop their behavior or risk arrest.[30]

The prosecution maintained that Sheriff Sixkiller and his deputies unfairly targeted Jeter Thompson out of all the unruly men involved in the incident. After both sides of the case were presented, the matter was turned over to the jury. The jury was unable to reach a decision, and the case was referred to the Council Branch of the National Council of the Cherokee Nation.[31] The tribe's legislative branch consisted of a fifteen-member tribal council representing various districts of the Cherokee

Nation and was overseen by the newly appointed Principal Chief of the Cherokee people, Dennis Wolfe Bushyhead. A full investigation by the council showed that Sheriff Sixkiller was in the right. According to a letter written by Chief Bushyhead to the lower court dated November 14, 1879, "The Council Branch of the National Council failed to find any proof that would implicate Sam Sixkiller as guilty of murder and malpractice in office as charged; therefore the charges were ignored by a majority vote of the body."[32]

Although there are no records that explain why Jeter Thompson believed Sheriff Sixkiller would choose to persecute him, historians speculate the issue might extend back to the Trail of Tears. Thompson's family supported John Ross and those who were opposed to leaving the Cherokee homeland no matter what the government promised. Sixkiller's ancestors were more inclined to side with John Ridge, who was in favor of relocating for a price. Some Indians felt the Lighthorsemen, even years after the treaty between the Cherokee Nation and the US government was signed, punished and arrested only Cherokee people who agreed with John Ross and had opposed the move from their homeland.[33]

Sheriff Sixkiller was relieved by the outcome of the hearing, but he was still angry over being forced out of his job as High Sheriff. He demanded lost wages from the more than five months of suspension and asked the council to pay his attorneys' fees as well. His back wages amounted to $355.50 and the cost for the team of lawyers was $975.[34]

The council offered to reinstate the sheriff to his former position in law enforcement and as warden of the prison, but they refused to pay what he felt he was owed. Believing the council's actions and the stigma of the trial itself would make it impossible for him to be effective at his job in Tahlequah, the sheriff declined the offer. Those who never doubted Sheriff Sixkiller's integrity were opposed to him leaving and pleaded with him to stay, but he could not be persuaded to change his mind.[35]

By early February 1880 Sheriff Sixkiller had moved his family to Muskogee. The raucous cow town was growing rapidly and was in need of fearless men to rein in the lawlessness sweeping across the sprawling burg. Sheriff Sixkiller was hired to bring about order.[36]

4

Mayhem in Muskogee

Captain Sixkiller is always the right man at the right place.
—*Indian Journal*, August 11, 1881

A hot sun beat down on the busy residents of Muskogee, Oklahoma Territory, in June 1880. A heavy veil of humidity, like a stifling blanket, hung over the town as well.[1] Situated nearly thirty miles southwest of Tahlequah, the primitive railroad stop was slowly coming into its own. More than five hundred people called the area home, and many among them were employees of the Missouri Pacific Railroad. At the end of the day, workers gathered by the score and milled about the hamlet of lean-tos, tents, and cabins. Gamblers had pitched their canvas dwellings in prime spots, and crowds flocked around their tables. Quarrels frequently flared up between slick poker dealers and inexperienced card players. Soiled doves (prostitutes) prowled around the gaming tents and curious male bystanders like panthers. They enticed men to their crude rooms, then stripped them of any funds they had not already lost in a crooked card game. Unsuspecting shoppers and their families roamed in and out of the heated arguments that spilled into the street, gawking warily at the chaos while on their way to and from various stores.[2]

City officials watched the scene play out in disgust. Bootleg alcohol was usually sold to the railroad crews and the houses of ill repute, and the clientele had a hard time controlling the amount they consumed. More often than not, customers who frequented bawdy houses and who drank to excess were prone to violence.[3] They terrorized the neighborhood surrounding the brothels, recklessly firing their guns at women and children and brawling with townsmen who challenged them to put away their weapons.[4]

In spite of repeat warnings from law enforcement officers like Colonel J. Q. Tuffts, a US agent for the Union Indian Agency in Muskogee, the madams who ran the brothels refused to voluntarily shut down their businesses. Brothels were considered a necessary evil; after all, a portion of the income spent at these houses supported public services such as the police department.[5] Nevertheless, Agent Tuffts considered the bordellos a plague on the town, nothing more than a refuge for criminals and delinquents from miles around. When Agent Tuffts made Sheriff Sixkiller captain of the Indian Police in early February 1880, he made ridding Muskogee of such houses a priority for Sam's administration.[6] Anxious to prove himself in Muskogee since leaving office under a cloud of turmoil in Tahlequah, Sixkiller was eager to accept the job and the challenge.[7]

According to the July 12, 1880, edition of the *Indian Journal,* Captain Sixkiller and seven deputies, representing the entire body of the police force, marched through the streets of Muskogee to a house in the red light district occupied by the most sought-after working women in town. A sign in front of the structure read Hotel de Adams.[8] Captain Sixkiller and his men stopped short of the building and studied their next move carefully. A couple of cattle punchers tromped out of the enterprising establishment and headed off in the opposite direction of the lawmen, unaware anything out of the ordinary was about to happen. Laughter wafted out through the open windows of the building. Captain Sixkiller motioned for deputies on his left and right to cover the back of the business. After giving the men sufficient time to get into place, he moved up the dusty path and through the front door with the remaining lawmen.[9]

The startled female occupants of the hotel screamed and cursed at the police raiding the bordello. Some threw chamber pots, hand mirrors, and other small objects at the men. Half-dressed patrons quickly fled the scene, unconcerned about the possibility of leaving personal items behind. Captain Sixkiller and the other officers led the women out of the hotel at gunpoint. The more seasoned prostitutes were furious and shouted out their protests as they were escorted to the jail. Controlling the angry ladies was a major undertaking—the women spit at and scratched any lawman that came too close.[10]

Once the soiled doves were securely locked in the cells, the rattled police force inspected the cuts and bruises they had incurred. Captain Sixkiller later confessed to family and friends that he would have "rather gone up against a band of desperate outlaws." The captain gave the fallen women a choice to leave town or remain in jail. Much to the approval of Agent Tufts, they chose to leave Muskogee.[11]

In December 1886 Robert L. Owens, an agent for the Five Civilized Tribes, suggested the law against keeping houses of ill fame should include the following warning: "Women of the 'baser sort' plying their vocation and their houses are often the rendezvous of reckless men, who carry deadly weapons, and who become involved in broils, and shoot off their pistols, and terrorize the neighborhood."[12]

Prostitution was just one of many illegal activities Captain Sixkiller had to contend with as the head of the Union Agency police force. His specific duties were to "preserve order by arresting thieves and violators of US law, suppressing the whiskey traffic, and executing the orders of the Indian agent." The February 12, 1880, edition of the *Indian Journal* praised Agent Tufft's appointment of Captain Sixkiller to the Muskogee jurisdiction. "There is a very noticeable improvement," the article noted about the duties Sixkiller had already performed during his short tenure in town. "We are all quiet now and we hope to remain so."[13]

Captain Sixkiller earned eight dollars a month, and the men under his command earned five dollars. Aware that the wages were small, Agent Tuffts allowed members of the police force to supplement their income by taking jobs as guards for coal-mining companies, drawing expense money for removing white intruders (also known as boomers) on Indian land, or working as special agents for the railroads. Captain Sixkiller hired on as an agent for the Missouri Pacific Railroad, one of the first railroads in the United States west of the Mississippi River.[14]

The Missouri Pacific Railroad was under the control of the highly successful but extremely controversial New York financier, Jay Gould.[15] Gould was the leading railroad executive in America and one of the country's wealthiest businessmen. In 1863 he purchased the Rutland & Washington Railway and in 1867 became the director of the Erie Railroad. His business tactics were less than honest. He speculated in securities on smaller rail lines, engaged in outrageous financial manipulation, issued fraudulent stock, and bribed government officials to legalize worthless paper. Upon acquiring control of the Union Pacific Railroad in 1881, he became the owner of the largest railroad empire in the United States. Gould was often referred to as a "robber baron," a pejorative term used for powerful businessmen or bankers who used questionable practices to acquire their power or wealth.[16]

The railroad paid Captain Sixkiller twelve hundred dollars a year to help keep survey parties and track layers safe from attack by warring Indians. He and the other agents working with him also protected the railroad from being hijacked or robbed by thieves. The exceptional job Captain Sixkiller had done running the jail in Tahlequah from 1874 to 1879 prompted Agent Tuffts to place him in charge of the new two-story prison in Muskogee in 1880. Sam doubted he would have trouble finding inmates to house at the facility.[17]

In addition to his position as an agent for the railroad, top man of the Union Agency police force, and warden of the Muskogee jail, thirty-eight-year-old Captain Sixkiller was commissioned by Judge Isaac Parker to be a US deputy marshal. However varied his duties were, his allegiance was always to keeping the peace in Muskogee, which had a reputation as one of the most dangerous towns in the untamed area.[18] During the frontier era more lawmen were killed in a fifty-mile radius of Muskogee than anywhere west of the Mississippi River. Men like Willis Pettit hoped to add Captain Sixkiller to the list of fatalities. Sam had arrested Pettit on assault charges when he was sheriff of Tahlequah. Pettit had served time in jail, but that had not persuaded him to change his ways. He was a drifter with a bad temper, usually armed and vowing to kill any lawmen who dared to take him in again for his misdeeds. But the captain couldn't be intimidated.[19]

On October 14, 1881, Captain Sixkiller apprehended Pettit in Muskogee for attempting to kill a horse trader named Henry Bird. Unhappy with the deal he was offered for a pair of stolen mules, Pettit stabbed Bird in the back. According to witnesses at the scene of the crime, Bird wasn't fast enough to get out of reach of the agitated Pettit. Bird was taken to a local doctor, and Pettit was taken into custody without incident.[20]

Earlier in the same month, Captain Sixkiller had arrested a farmer named Henry Blake for assault with a deadly weapon. Blake had shot and wounded fellow farmer Warner Bruner while two people looked on. Bruner reportedly was discussing corn with the two men when Blake approached him with a gun and fired.[21] No motive was given for his actions.

The majority of lawbreakers Captain Sixkiller dealt with were men, but occasionally women were involved in crimes as well. Such was the case in late October 1881. Captain Sixkiller, along with Chief Deputy J. M. Huffington of Fort Worth, Texas, combined forces to track down two lady bootleggers known as Cunningham and Annie. The women

Trackbeds like the ones being built for the Missouri-Pacific Railroad dotted the landscape across Indian land. Captain Sixkiller was hired as a special agent to protect the railroad from being robbed. COURTESY OF THE RESEARCH DIVISION OF THE OKLAHOMA HISTORICAL SOCIETY

were operating a store ten miles northeast of Muskogee and selling large quantities of whiskey to customers in addition to the usual grocery items such as coffee and beans. Numerous deputies had been called to the scene but could never find the liquor, and without it there was no evidence to convict. Because there was big money to be made by bootleggers, offenders were constantly developing schemes to hide their product from the law.[22]

Every method one could imagine had been concocted. For example, some bootleggers would affix a long tube to a barrel of cheap whiskey, bury the cask with the tube extending just aboveground, then scatter seeds on the dirt that, once grown, would cover all evidence of the burial. To extract the liquid, a quart syringe was affixed to the protruding tube and the whiskey could be transferred to a glass or jug. The barrel was never approached the same way by more than one person, so as not to leave a path. Unfortunately for the bootleggers, though, the vigilance of the deputies kept pace with the ingenuity of the outlaws, and it was only a question of time before the latter would be transferred to jail.[23]

According to the September 9, 1894, edition of the *Galveston Daily News,* on that day in October Captain Sam Sixkiller and Chief Huffington rode out to the store to see what they could learn. The two women had been operating the same type of business in the Fort Worth area, and Chief Huffington had tracked the pair to Oklahoma.[24]

The store was a plain log house, and it was located near a small creek but out on the open prairie. Cunningham, the leader of the two, was a large, fleshy, white woman with black eyes. Annie was a small, slender, athletic-looking Indian woman. The women would have nothing to do with the lawmen when they arrived. They acted annoyed when asked if they would sell the men whiskey. Each shook their head, and Cunningham denied any knowledge of liquor around her place. "Ain't you fellas tired of pestering an old widow?" Cunningham reportedly asked the lawmen. "I'm sure tired of it! You both better get out of here!" she demanded. Annie said nothing.

"Madam, we know you do sell whiskey, and we have the proper papers for the purpose and we propose to find where the whiskey is," Huffington announced. "Well, I ain't never had a drop of whiskey in the house and your men have searched here enough to find that out, goodness knows," Cunningham snapped back. "But maybe you'll be smart enough now to find out what never was or isn't, so crack your whip."

The two officers thoroughly searched the business. They hunted up and down the chimney; over, under, and in the beds; in trunks and the stove; and over and under the house. The women jeered the men as they investigated every possible hiding spot. For three hours they searched the house and down the creek, and then Captain Sixkiller remarked, "Well, it beats me. What do you think?" Huffington replied, "I'm badly rattled, Six, but that whiskey is somewhere, and don't let's give up. Say, Six, I've got an idea. We have checked everything around this cabin but not the logs used to build the place?"

The two went to work, Captain Sixkiller searching the logs on the interior wall of the cabin and Huffington doing the same on the outside of the structure. Huffington's exterior search of the building was a bust and he joined the Captain inside the cabin to help. After a time Captain Sixkiller noticed a few calico dresses oddly out of place hanging on a wall. When he removed them, he discovered what appeared to be a little plug or chip in the seventh log from the floor. When he tapped the log from the inside, it gave a peculiar half-metallic sound. He pried away the chip and found that it was mortised in, the work done so precisely as to deceive the practical eye. Its removal disclosed a small faucet.

So eager had Huffington been to unveil the find that he completely forgot the women were still in the room with them. When he called out to Captain Sixkiller, a deafening report rang out and a .45 slug buried itself in the log before him, missing his head by about half an inch. Quickly turning and drawing his weapon, he discovered that he had no use for it, as Captain Sixkiller had already drawn his weapon. Suddenly Annie wrenched the pistol from Cunningham and turned it over to Captain Sixkiller. Both of the women were placed under arrest.

The bullet fired at Huffington did its work. From the hole spurted a stream of whiskey. An examination revealed two hollow, copper-lined logs that each held over a barrel of whiskey. A stretched coonskin on the outside hid the outer aperture, which was fitted to a large, detachable funnel.

The two women were taken to Fort Smith. Their sentence was suspended provided they leave Indian country for good, which they consented to do.[25]

Crimes committed by white men on Indian land, or offenses against law enforcement that were perpetrated by Indians against white men or while accompanied by white men, could not be handled by the Indian courts. Felons falling in that category had to go before a federal judge.[26] After Judge Isaac Parker of the Western District of Arkansas recommended that Captain Sixkiller be given a commission as a US deputy marshal in 1880, the captain brought many accused men and women before the notorious "hanging judge." Parker had earned the title because of the strict punishment he handed down to convicted offenders. It wasn't uncommon for him to order several convicted felons to be hanged at one time on a long scaffolding constructed specifically for the job.[27]

From March 1880 to December 1886, Captain Sixkiller and his deputies investigated numerous murders and attempted murders. Most homicides were not premeditated, but were the result of spur-of-the-moment arguments that got out of control. In late winter 1881 a Choctaw Indian named Nathan Harris was shot down by three white men as they were leaving a public wrestling match. The white men accused Harris of cursing at them as they exited the event. Captain Sixkiller had the task of arresting the murderers and transporting them to Fort Smith, Arkansas, to stand before Judge Isaac Parker.[28] The March 11, 1881, edition of the *Indian Journal* praised the captain's ability to perform his job so efficiently and courageously. "Sixkiller occupies a position for which he is well qualified—captain of the Indian police—and is a terror to evildoers," the article boasted.[29]

That same month the lawman turned over five more violent prisoners to the US court in Arkansas: Frank Webster, charged with assault; Gus Barron, charged with murder; and Henry Lewis, James Murphy, and Nancy Britton, each charged with larceny. He also transported a well-known and elusive highwayman named Bill Rider safely to Fort Smith.[30]

In August 1881 William R. Fox shot and wounded two brothers (identified in Fox's arrest records only by their last name of Arnold) over a card game. Fox had been drinking and was thought to be drunk when he picked up a gun and started shooting. He was held over for trial and found guilty of assault with intent to kill.[31] On October 7, 1881, Charles Buffington shot and killed Robert Mahon over a disagreement involving wild game. Again the *Indian Journal* recognized the captain for the good work he was doing. "Captain Sixkiller is always at the right place at the right time," the October 11, 1881, edition noted.[32]

There were times when Muskogee law enforcement officials erroneously suspected known criminals of deliberately setting out to kill anyone with whom they had a conflict. Frank Woods was one such man. According to the writ (an order from the court) signed by Captain Sixkiller on January 15, 1882, Woods "feloniously, willfully, and with premeditation, malice and forethought killed and murdered one Nathan Johnson, a white man." Shortly after Johnson's demise a physician was called in to examine the body. He determined that prior to the date the man expired, he'd received several blows to the head with a blunt instrument. Captain Sixkiller went on a fact-finding mission. Johnson's friends and family suggested that Woods struck Johnson in the head repeatedly with a pistol and took the alcohol he had on him. Woods admitted to being with Johnson before he died but insisted he never touched him. He claimed the man was drunk and fell against his house.[33]

Witnesses for Woods reported that the two men had minimal difficulties between them and that Woods did not have a pistol. They testified that prior to the discovery of the body, Woods had wandered off drunk sometime during the evening without anyone knowing. With nothing more concrete to present to the courts, Captain Sixkiller was forced to discharge Woods.[34]

Stealing a horse was one of the most serious offenses Captain Sixkiller had to handle. Taking a man's horse generally left the victim with no way to maintain his livelihood.[35] In some states, such as Texas, thieves could be lynched for the act. When the captain arrested Charles Ashcroft for stealing a horse in February 1882, Ashcroft was at risk of being sentenced to the gallows. Four witnesses saw him lead his neighbor's horse (estimated to be worth seventy-five dollars) out of town. The captain brought Ashcroft before Judge Isaac Parker. (There are no records to indicate what kind of punishment Ashcroft received from the judge.)[36]

After Captain Sixkiller returned from delivering Ashcroft and a few other convicts to the high court at Fort Smith, he dealt with a lawbreaker in Muskogee named Frank Jones. Authorities were uncertain what Frank's last name really was because he was uncertain of it himself. Most of the time the man went by the name of Jones, but he also referred to himself as Frank Cleburn.[37]

Frank was a simple-minded man who frequently brought liquor onto Indian land to sell. In September 1882 he was caught stealing a pistol from a mercantile in town. The value of the gun was fifteen dollars. Captain Sixkiller apprehended Frank and held him over for trial in Muskogee. He was found guilty, sentenced to time already served, ordered to return the pistol to its rightful owner, and levied a hefty fine.[38]

The railroads that crisscrossed Indian land did more than connect thriving populations—they also provided criminals with new ways to break the law. As a law enforcement agent for the Missouri Pacific Railroad, Captain Sixkiller frequently encountered desperados who robbed or attempted to rob the train. The Katy, as the Missouri Pacific Railroad was more commonly referred to (derived from its former name of Missouri-Kansas-Texas Railroad), was held up more often than any other rail line. The Katy line went through many of the territories occupied by the Five Civilized Tribes. As a result of the treaty the federal government had agreed upon, the tribes received regular cash disbursements via the Katy.[39] Train robbers had a difficult time resisting the temptation of all this money being transported from the capital to stops in Oklahoma Territory. Barney Sweeny was one of those robbers.

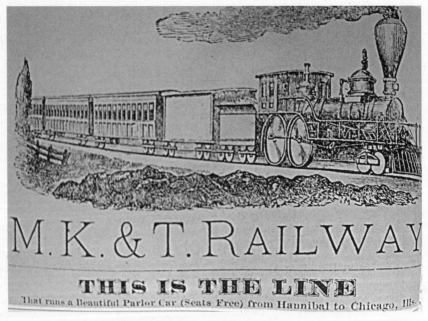

The Missouri-Kansas-Texas Railroad traveled through the Indian Nations protected by special agents like Captain Sixkiller. AUTHOR'S COLLECTION

On September 9, 1882, Sweeny warned railroad officials that there was going to be a holdup of the train at a depot in Vinita, Oklahoma Territory, a town near Muskogee. Sweeny claimed the plan to rob the train had been orchestrated by two petty thieves. According to the January 20, 1888, edition of the *New York Times*, Sweeny reported that Jim Cunningham and William Wilson had approached him and asked him to act as decoy and informer. The three men were to be stationed on the train. Sweeny was to be at one end and Wilson at the other. Cunningham would be in the car where the money was kept. "The officials prepared for the alleged train robbery and watched carefully as Sweeny designated the car Cunningham would be on," the *New York Times* noted.[40]

When the train pulled into Vinita, Sweeny went to the platform of the baggage car and was soon joined by the conductor, a man named Chick Warner, and Wilson. As soon as the conductor entered the car, Sweeny covered him with his revolver. Without saying a word Sweeny suddenly turned and shot Wilson, putting three bullets into him after he had fallen. Afterward it was learned that Sweeney had designed the whole scheme to "get even with Wilson for taking his share of the money they had stolen on another robbery."[41]

Sweeny not only killed William Wilson but also took the conductor's money and watch. Before he fled the scene, he shot the conductor in the jaw, killing him too. Thomas Furlong, the chief detective for the railroad, requested a "special commission to bring Sweeny down."[42] Captain Sixkiller was notified at once about the incident and the criminal at large. The captain telegraphed marshals at Fort Smith and let them know that he, Furlong, and two other railroad agents would be departing Muskogee at once to find the fugitive and arrest him.

Unfortunately, although the captain tried to hide the fact, he was suffering with a fever and, just as preparations were being made to pursue Sweeny, he collapsed. Sixkiller was escorted to a doctor, who informed Furlong that the captain was confined to bed with a severe attack of fever.[43]

"Upon receipt of this information, I reported to Luke Sixkiller, a brother of the chief, who lived at Vinita, and who was a member of the United States police force," Furlong recalled later in his memoirs. "I requested Luke to accompany me to where Sweeny was living with his brother-in-law to arrest him. Luke promptly told me he would not dare arrest Sweeny unless his brother, the chief, was present. 'Why,' he said, 'this man Sweeny is a terror. He is a wonderful shot with either rifle or pistol, and it will take at least a half-dozen men, well-armed, to capture him. He is a desperate man, and so we will have to wait until the Chief gets well enough to come and help capture him.'"[44]

Sweeny was indeed a terror. He was a member of Jesse James's gang, had taken part in many train robberies, and was suspected of murdering four men. But Furlong wasn't intimated by Sweeny's record. He tracked him to a shack near Little Cabin Creek and arrested him. Furlong escorted Sweeny back to Vinita, and Captain Sixkiller, who left his sickbed to assist in the arrest, met the men at the depot. He had heard there would be trouble taking Sweeny to jail and warned Furlong not to take the outlaw through Muskogee. The conductor that Sweeny killed was very popular among the employees of the railroad, and those employees were threatening violence. Furlong boarded a train to St. Louis and, with Sweeny, traveled to Arkansas.[45]

By September 22, 1882, less than two weeks after the incident, the culprit was in custody. "Barney Sweeny, the man who gave information regarding the recent attempted train robbery near Muskogee, and who was credited with having helped to frustrate the scheme, has been arrested," the Iola, Kansas, newspaper, the *Iola Register*, read. Sweeny was then bound over by a grand jury at Fort Smith and scheduled to stand trial on February 5, 1883.[46]

Railroad executives praised Captain Sixkiller for his dedication to the job and for thwarting a vigilante attack on the accused. The captain's health steadily improved, and he returned to his many law enforcement duties in early October 1882.[47]

5

Defending the Nation

I verily believe that the Cherokee are the most moral, happy, law abiding and prosperous Nation on earth.
—Comment by a special correspondent observing the Indians in the Oklahoma Territory while on assignment for the Petersburg Daily News, February 7, 1887

A springboard wagon topped a ridge surrounded by a grove of ancient juniper trees seven miles outside Muskogee. The wagon was weighted down with several heavy crates and made little sound. The contents inside the crates sloshed as the vehicle slogged through the rain-soaked turf. The soft ground muffled the hardworking wheels and the horses' hooves. Solomon Coppell, an unshaven man dressed in a dirty, fawn-colored suit with a long-tailed coat, drove the wagon over a crude trail cut deep in mud and dirt. His roving button eyes scanned the scene in front of him, looking for anything out of the ordinary.

Just beyond Solomon's line of sight, tucked behind a thicket of brush, Captain Sam Sixkiller sat on his horse watching the driver.[1] Sweat rolled down the lawman's face that late spring day in 1883 as the sun rode up into a leaden sky, empty and cloudless, and blanketed the captain with a sticky heat. Solomon was uncomfortable too. He pulled his flat-brimmed hat off his head, backhanded a bead of perspiration off his hairline, reset his hat, and fixed his gaze back on the muddy track.[2] The captain waited for just the right moment, and in one fast, flawless movement spurred his horse onto the trail directly in front of Solomon's team.

A stunned Solomon quickly jerked back on the reins of the animals, bringing the skittish horses to a stop. "Hold it, Coppell!" Captain Sixkiller announced in a sober, stern voice. "You're under arrest." Solomon glanced at the cargo he was hauling and back to the captain. The lawman was alone and the bootlegger was confident he could survive a confrontation with his wagonload intact. Solomon stared at the captain for a moment, then shook his head. "I got a tip you were bringing booze into the Nation," the captain informed him. Solomon didn't reply and showed no signs of cooperating. "Surrender, Coppell," Captain Sixkiller warned him again. "Throw your guns out in the road."

The captain was empty-handed, his leg gun still resting in a holster on his thigh. Coppell made a grab for the shotgun on the wagon seat. Sixkiller's hand whipped forward in a short, small arc. There was no strain. He saw Coppell's face, distorted and desperate. His gun kicked back against his wrist. One shot. Captain Sixkiller's gun exploded before it cleared his coat. The flame of the lawman's shot licked through the fabric and curled to form a smoldering ring. He watched Coppell's body jerk. Coppell swayed and fell into the trace chains and wagon tongue. The team reared and snorted and pawed at the air. The captain calmed the horses and kept them from running away.[3]

Most Muskogee residents agreed that Captain Sixkiller was an effective policeman, quick to enforce the laws regarding the buying and selling of liquor. Nevertheless, some thought the rules should be relaxed. Cherokee Indian business owners believed they should have the right to purchase liquor to sell to white railroad workers and settlers passing through. Indian leaders maintained that such measures would lead to an increase in violence on the Cherokee Nation and insisted that troublemakers who peddled whiskey needed to be stopped.[4]

Although Captain Sixkiller was never accused of being too harsh on those who violated the law, some Indians, including former chief of the Cherokee Nation, Lewis Downing, and Indian agent John B. Jones, thought that the US marshal and his deputies went too far in upholding the law. "Some deputy marshals make forcible arrests," Chief Downing told Indian agent Jones in a letter, "without regard to circumstances or the facts of the case, and without any of the forms of law."[5] Smugglers occasionally planted whiskey on innocent people traveling through the Cherokee Nation. If they were stopped by Captain Sixkiller or his deputies and alcohol was found in their possession, they were arrested and taken immediately to Fort Smith, Arkansas, to be prosecuted. Chief Downing strenuously objected to the captain's rush to judgment, arguing that in those instances, such individuals should be given the benefit of the doubt.[6]

Captain Sixkiller's primary focus, however, was on legitimate lawbreakers. Solomon Coon had run afoul of the lawman on several occasions for introducing spirituous liquors into Indian country. On February 20, 1883, Coon expanded his illegal activities to include the theft of thirty sacks of flour and twelve boxes of cigars. The value of the items was estimated to be more than seventy dollars. The flour and cigars had been reported stolen by the railroad company. A railroad detective, who spotted Coon hanging around the depot in Muskogee, suspected he was responsible for the items disappearing and shared the information with Captain Sixkiller.[7]

The lawman proceeded to Solomon's home and told him of the suspicions. "I explained to him that I wanted to see if he had acquired any flour that night," the captain wrote in his arrest statement. "He took me to the back room and showed me the flour." Coon claimed the flour was given to him by parties unknown. Captain Sixkiller suspected Coon was going to use the flour to make a topping to cover the barrels of homemade whiskey also found at his home during the investigation. The man was arrested for receiving and concealing stolen property and introducing spirituous liquor in the Indian Country.[8]

Captain Sixkiller rarely met bootleggers as cooperative as Solomon Coon. In the summer of 1883, the lawman encountered a group of brothers, known as the Lee boys, selling whiskey at a spot along the Arkansas River. The alcohol was being sold by the glass, bottle, or barrel. The four men transported the goods via wagon, with two riding on the vehicle and two on horseback in front keeping a lookout for the police. They were known to be armed with Winchester rifles and six-shooters. According to an article in the March 1883 edition of the *Indian Journal,* Captain Sixkiller received a dispatch from a US marshal at Fort Smith to be on the lookout for the Lee boys. When they would be in the area was anyone's guess, but Fort Smith authorities wanted Captain Sixkiller and his men to be on guard. More than two years would pass before the lawman and the Lee boys' paths would cross.[9]

Brothers James, Tom, and Pink Lee owned a ranch in the Chickasaw Nation but weren't interested in finding their own animals to raise and sell. They coveted their neighbor's stock and devised a plan to steal it. In April 1885 the Lee brothers, along with a few other miscreants, rode onto the Roff brothers' ranch in the dead of night and drove off their livestock. Before sunrise the gang of men had the animals corralled at the Lee property. On May 1, 1885, a posse was formed to track the Lee gang and take back the stolen horses and cows. The animals were retrieved, but not before several of the gang members died in a gun battle. The Lee brothers escaped before the authorities burned down their house in an attempt to smoke the desperados out of the building. The law finally caught up to Tom. He was sent to Fort Smith, Arkansas, to stand trial. James and Pink remained at large.[10]

James and Pink Lee left Texas and headed into Oklahoma Territory. In August 1885, news that the brothers and two of their associates were last seen riding toward Muskogee reached Captain Sixkiller. They were not only reportedly armed with Winchester rifles but also selling barrels of whiskey to cattlemen. James drove the wagon filled with liquor, and

Pink and the other two members of the gang followed along on either side of the vehicle to spot anyone looking for them.

Captain Sixkiller had an idea where the men could ultimately be found and told the officers working with him that "capture was not improbable." The lawman and his deputies hurried out of Muskogee past the town of Vinita on their way to the ford of the Verdigris River. Captain Sixkiller hoped they would reach the river before the Lee brothers crossed, but unfortunately that was not the case. The outlaws were already riding through the prairie on the other side when Captain Sixkiller caught sight of them.[11]

The Lee brothers were afraid of being caught by Sixkiller, so they turned around and started back toward the river so they could hide in the dense trees lining the water. A violent storm rolled in and deluged the renegades and the lawmen holed up on either side of the river.

The following morning Captain Sixkiller made it across the river, but the Lee gang had already ridden out. The captain determined they had fled in the middle of the night with the storm still raging around them. The rain washed away any tracks that otherwise would have been left behind. According to the *Indian Journal,* "They had seven good horses," reported Captain Sixkiller about the outlaws. "They hid their whiskey and left their wagon in their haste to get away," he added.[12] The captain continued after the Lee brothers, vowing not to return to Muskogee until the criminals were caught. The Lee brothers were killed on September 7, 1885, near Lake Texoma, seven miles north of Dexter, Texas, by lawmen Heck Thomas, Jim Taylor, and Jim Shattles. The two remaining members of the gang were apprehended in Dennison, Texas.[13] Captain Sixkiller rode back to Oklahoma Territory shortly after he learned of the outlaws' demise.[14] The captain's experience with the Lee boys was covered fully by newspapers in 1885 after Sixkiller described the event to a reporter with the *Indian Journal.*[15]

As a US marshal, Captain Sixkiller frequently transported various criminals to Fort Smith. In late winter 1883 his trips to Arkansas served a dual purpose: Not only was he escorting outlaws to the jail there, but he also was keeping tabs on a trial involving a fellow police officer named Sam Paul. Paul was a well-respected man and a friend of the captain. In mid-March 1883 Paul had been part of a posse searching for a gang of horse thieves. Two of the gang members, brothers John and William Hawkins, were quickly apprehended. The gang leaders, known only as Cox and Sturdevant, remained at large.[16]

In the hope of eliciting information from the brothers that might lead them to the whereabouts of Cox and Sturdevant, Paul decided to isolate the men and question them separately. Paul was interrogating John Hawkins when the outlaw lunged at the lawman and grabbed a rifle from him. John fired at Paul and missed. Paul drew his six-shooter and shot John.[17] Seriously wounded, John tried to flee the scene but fell down a brush-covered embankment. Paul chased the suspect, but by the time he reached him, John was dead. The posse returned to town with William Hawkins and reported the casualty.

William was convicted of stealing livestock and sentenced to serve time at the prison at Fort Smith. Once he was released, he filed charges against Paul for the death of his brother. William claimed he and John were purposely separated the day of their capture and arrest so Paul could kill John. He further claimed that Paul had confessed to killing John while the latter was on his knees begging for his life. Paul was taken into custody and made to stand trial.[18]

On March 26, 1883, Captain Sixkiller returned to Muskogee from Fort Smith with positive news about Paul. The *Indian Journal* shared the information with the community in a small article on the front page. "Captain Sixkiller reports the Sam Paul case as being called on the day he left (Friday) with all the witnesses on hand. He says the case is looking more hopeful than heretofore mentioned. We who live in this section think it strange that Paul should confess to such a hideous crime to parties with whom he never was very intimate."[19]

The jury was split in their decision. Six jurors believed Paul was guilty of manslaughter and six thought he was innocent. He spent nine months in jail before he was officially acquitted.[20] Sam Paul returned to work as a lawman in 1884 and assisted Captain Sixkiller in helping to apprehend a bootlegger known as Isaac Deer.[21]

Laws restricting the possession of any beverage that could negatively affect or influence Indians were strictly enforced. Captain Sixkiller and his men were mandated to confiscate not only whiskey and beer, but also "hard cider and ginger." But liquor regulations established by the US government regarding Indians could only be enforced in Indian country. American settlements outside those areas came under state jurisdiction. Members of the Five Civilized Tribes could go across the borders, enter neighboring towns, and return to their own nation with liquor.[22]

Indians initially regarded liquor like any other item they could trade for at outposts operated by white settlers. Any liquor they could acquire either through a store or by making themselves (using a mixture of natural roots and herbs) was only to be used as a ceremonial beverage. As more and more native people began to drink liquor outside of those settings, the problems with drunkenness started to occur. Indians leaders maintained that large quantities of liquor in any form impaired the decision-making process. Chiefs and elders enacted laws to suppress drunkenness among their citizens. Such laws included eliminating spirituous liquors from public events and prohibiting spirituous liquors within three miles of the General Council House or at any courthouse during General Council meetings. Lighthorsemen were authorized to confiscate and destroy any liquor discovered.[23]

Not every Indian agreed with the strict policy. Cherokee such as Isaac Deer were convinced that strong drinks fought disease and sickness and argued that "putting alcohol aside would be equivalent to denying our right to employ any substance whatever as a medicine." It was on the basis of this argument that he peddled whiskey to various tribes throughout

Oklahoma Territory. After reading an ad in the *Detroit Free Press* entitled "Whiskey—a Medicine," Deer became interested in preaching the "judicious use of alcoholic stimulants."[24]

When Captain Sixkiller arrested Isaac Deer on May 10, 1884, for theft, Deer tried to sell the lawman on the folly of attempting to rid the Cherokee Nation of alcohol. He described how if an Indian wanted to drink, he had to leave Oklahoma Territory and venture into Arkansas or Missouri, where it was legal. Deer told the captain the idea was ridiculous and inconvenient to most people. He insisted that he provided a valuable service to his fellow Indians.

Captain Sixkiller charged Deer with "feloniously stealing, taking and carrying away the good and chattels (property) of one T. J. Wrightman." After sampling some of his own "medicinal drinks," Deer had stolen a bale of hides valued at twenty-five dollars from Wrightman. He was found guilty of the crime in September 1884 and sentenced to eighteen months in the House of Corrections in Detroit.[25]

Oftentimes Captain Sixkiller would personally escort condemned felons from the Muskogee area to the location where they would be serving their sentences. In November 1884, after leading two prisoners who had been convicted of selling alcohol to the jail in Tahlequah, he decided to stop to rest at an eatery there before returning home. The stop led to the arrest of yet another bootlegger. The November 20, 1884, edition of the *Indian Journal* reported that Captain Sixkiller was sitting at a business called Taylors at sunset when a suspicious-looking young man entered. "The youth came up, without seeing the captain and asked Taylor (the owner of the establishment) if he wanted a few quarts," the article began. "Taylor said yes, and the young man said he would meet him at the stables at 8 o'clock. When he arrived he met the captain instead and was promptly run in."[26]

The young man informed Captain Sixkiller that the bulk of the alcohol he had for sale was being stored at a creek nearby. Aided by the sheriff of Tahlequah and his deputy, the captain traveled the creek line a few miles away and soon came upon the peddler's headquarters. They searched a wagon there and found five gallons of whiskey. An old man guarding the alcohol claimed the young man selling the liquor was acting on his own. Captain Sixkiller didn't believe the gentleman. He arrested the man and confiscated the wagon. The young peddler told the lawman his name was Jon Copper and added he was from Tennessee. He begged the lawman to take the whiskey and let him go. The captain refused.[27]

Professionally things were going well for Captain Sixkiller. He had tracked down and apprehended numerous lawbreakers, had collected thousands of dollars in fines from bootleggers, and had thwarted several attempts to rob the railroad. But personally he was still struggling. Unintentionally, he hurt Fannie with the news that his affair with Mary Malissia Murphey resulted in a son, James Thomas Sixkiller, born on February 11, 1874. Fannie and the captain managed to work through the issue and remained married.[28]

Fannie worried about her husband's wellbeing whenever he had to travel outside the immediate area to hunt down a criminal. If he was gone too long, rumors he had been killed in the line of duty would begin to circulate. In April 1883 a false report of the captain's death had been telegraphed throughout the Cherokee Nation. Fannie learned of her husband's "demise" in the *Indian Journal*. Not long after the article was printed, she found out that he was alive and well. The local paper was quick to report the updated news. "Captain Sixkiller came up from the Chickasaw Nation Monday looking fatter than ever in spite of the story of his death . . . evidently started by horse thieves," the report in the April 12, 1883, edition of the *Indian Journal* read. "While the captain was out at eleven o'clock at night three men came along heavily armed and inquired the way south. Being told, they got a drink and left, and the next morning parties who met them about fifteen miles south were told by them that Captain Sixkiller had been killed by horse thieves and they were on the track of the murderers. As the country was full of officers they told this to save themselves from molestation.[29]

"They must have continued with the same tale until they reached the Texas line, but as the captain did not know they had gone farther with it than to tell the first man they met, he did not take the trouble to write a denial, and he himself did not know how far the report ran until he reached the railroad."[30]

Captain Sixkiller and his force were always on the lookout for known train robbers rumored to be traveling through the Cherokee Nation. On January 29, 1885, the suspects were thought to be Frank and Jesse James.

Union Agency in Muskogee where Captain Sixkiller was chief of the Indian police. COURTESY OF THE RESEARCH DIVISION OF THE OKLAHOMA HISTORICAL SOCIETY

Governor Crittenden of Missouri passed the erroneous information about the James brothers on to Judge Isaac Parker, and he relayed the message to the captain. A five thousand dollar reward was being offered for the arrest and conviction of both men for the "train robberies near Winston and Glendale, Missouri and the murder of two men."[31] Apparently Jesse James's legend had outlived the man himself. He was never apprehended for the train robberies, having been assassinated by one of the members of his gang in April 1882. Frank James, who had surrendered to authorities for his criminal activities in October 1882, also escaped conviction for those particular crimes.

The Dalton Gang was another popular band of outlaws from Jackson County, Missouri, who specialized in bank and train robberies. They were suspected of being in the vicinity of Muskogee in 1885 and supposedly were contemplating robbing the Missouri Pacific Railroad outside of Vinita. Captain Sixkiller had encountered one of the nine members of the Dalton Gang, a man named Charlie Pierce, a couple of times during his career. Pierce was a whiskey peddler who had visited the Cherokee Nation with his liquor in tow and been chased off Indian land. Heck Thomas, another respected US deputy marshal, is credited with capturing the notorious bandits in 1892 after they attempted to rob a bank in Coffeyville, Kansas.[32]

Between traversing the countryside looking for outlaw gangs, Captain Sixkiller and the lawmen that served with him arrested a number of citizens who attempted to rebrand cattle belonging to intruders. Instead of reporting the settlers squatting on Indian land to authorities, some Cherokee and Chickasaw stole their livestock before driving the homesteaders on. In his monthly report to Indian leaders, Captain Sixkiller noted that more than "3,000 head of cattle had been taken and redistributed to various members of the tribe."[33]

On April 1, 1885, the captain and several other members of the Lighthorsemen tracked and apprehended three white men suspected in the derailment of a train near Colbert, Oklahoma, earlier in the year. Chick Kinney and William and James Allen, track layers for the Missouri Pacific Railroad, had a grievance with their employer about the pay they were receiving and wanted to retaliate. In addition to placing ties across the tracks, they also burned down a railroad bridge. The men were arrested at a tie camp outside the town of Armstrong, Oklahoma. They admitted their wrongdoing to Captain Sixkiller and gave him the names of the men they said aided them in their efforts. By the time the Lighthorsemen arrived at the spot where the accomplices were last seen, the criminals had fled the area. In an interview with the *Indian Journal* on April 8, 1885, the captain warned, "There is a bad gang about Colbert and they will have to go."[34]

In mid-1885 Captain Sixkiller had to divide his time between serious criminal offenses going on in the region and an increase in problems involving troublesome dogs. An article in the June 5, 1885, edition of the *Indian Journal* explained that a mad dog in Vinita had created a great deal of excitement. "Captain Sixkiller does not propose to have any wild or diseased canines around Muskogee," the story noted.[35] Try as he might to keep the problem of mad dogs contained, nothing worked. On June 11, 1885, the captain posted a notice in the *Indian Journal* about the matter that he hoped would help. "A warning is hereby given," the announcement began, "that all dogs found loose in Muskogee after Friday, June 18, without a muzzle will be promptly killed by the police. Dog owners will govern themselves accordingly."[36]

The demand of the many law enforcement jobs Captain Sixkiller was charged with was at times exhausting. He escaped the rigors of the position by hunting and camping. Oklahoma Territory politician Otto Beckmeyer frequently accompanied the lawman on these outings.[37] As with all the other activities in which the captain participated, the *Indian Journal* reported on the various ventures. "After their week's hunt," the April 23, 1885, article read, "the men returned with two or three gobblers and other game."[38]

Like most dedicated police officers of the untamed West, Captain Sixkiller was more satisfied traveling and pursuing lawbreakers than wild turkeys. A violent whiskey trader by the name of Dick Glass challenged the captain's public service talents and led him on a chase that spanned the entire Cherokee Nation in June 1885. The quest for Glass and his gang further solidified Captain Sixkiller's reputation as a fearless and committed officer of the law. It also reignited a long-standing dispute between the leaders of the Five Civilized Tribes and the African American people who were former slaves of the Muskogee Creek tribe and known as the Creek Freedmen.[39]

6

BADMAN DICK GLASS

Dick Glass is getting himself a name that will soon rival Jesse James.
— *MUSKOGEE PHOENIX*, APRIL 2, 1885

SHERIFF JOHN CULP AND CONSTABLE RUSH MEADOWS OF CHICK COUNTY, Texas, raced their foam-flecked horses into a dense stand of trees leading to the Arbuckle Mountains, several miles north of Muskogee. The seasoned riders guided their mounts around centuries-old pines and oaks, twisted with age, and massive boulders keeping company with the crowded forest.

The lawmen were in pursuit of the outlaw Dick Glass. Glass rode hard, maneuvering his horse in and out of downed timbers. An insane rage possessed him—he could not allow himself to be caught. He dug his heels into his ride and steered the animal toward an embankment. A wind that seemed to blow from the outer spaces of eternity swept his hat off. He didn't even glance after it.[1]

The one thousand dollar reward for Glass's capture, offered by the US Western District Federal Court, spurred the officers on.[2] Glass was a Creek Freedman—half Indian, half black—and a one-time farmer in the Creek Nation. When the Civil War ended in 1865, all the slaves belonging to Indians became free and equal. Generations of Creek Freedmen had been raised on the land they worked, and they wanted part of it for their own once the battle between the states had concluded. Not only was their request denied, but also they were dispossessed because they weren't Indian. Men like Dick Glass were bitter over the unjust treatment and many turned to a life of crime and retaliation.[3]

In late March 1885 Glass and the gang of miscreants that usually rode with him were run out of the Creek Nation for rustling cattle, stealing horses, and murdering. He reluctantly obliged, taking with him other Creek Freedmen who had partnered with him in his lawless activities.[4]

Glass roamed through the Seminole, Pottawatomie, and Chickasaw Nations to the Texas line before settling on a spot seven miles from Muskogee known as the Point. Glass and his gang made their way back to the Point after every criminal act. It was their rendezvous location, and lawmen who came looking and found him there never lived long enough to report it. There were no cabins, lean-tos, or barns on the property. Glass and the other desperados slept outdoors, exposed to the elements.[5]

The life of a renegade was tiring and uncomfortable; it was with this in mind that Glass decided to repent from his devious ways and set a new course. According to the letter he sent to the editors of the *Indian Journal* newspaper, to be posted on the front page, Glass "wished to become a law abiding citizen if the police would not molest him." The price already on his head, however, made the proposition impossible to accept.[6]

Texas lawmen Culp and Meadows were not swayed by Glass's promise to reform. They were going to bring him in regardless. For more than three months, they pushed on at a hard and steady gait through the rough terrain. After traveling more than 180 miles, the men brought their horses to a final halt in a clearing in the trees at the base of the mountains. Glass was sitting atop his nearly exhausted ride waiting for them. The lawmen approached the scene cautiously. A flash of satisfaction filled the sheriff's face as he surveyed the area for signs of anyone who might be coming to Glass's aid. Satisfied that Glass had simply given up, Culp ordered the outlaw to throw up his hands.[7] Glass had no intention of obliging. His hand streaked down toward the holster on his thigh. Sheriff Culp and Constable Meadows beat him to the draw and Glass was pitched off his horse.[8]

Once the smoke had cleared, the lawmen holstered their weapons and dismounted. They exchanged a congratulatory glance as they slowly approached the criminal lying in a heap on the ground. Glass was of average height and weight, with a scar running across the side of his neck from his ear down to his chest. It was a burn of some kind over which the skin had grown back red instead of black. A distinctive marking, it made it easy to recognize him in any situation. Glass also had a scar on one hand, made by a bullet that had passed through it during one of his shooting scrapes. Any fleeting doubt the lawmen might have had that the body lying motionless on the ground was anyone other than Glass was quickly put to rest.[9]

Just as Sheriff Culp bent down next to Glass to relieve him of his silver-plated guns with marble handles, the desperado popped his eyes open, jerked his guns out of their holsters, and fired twice. Both lawmen fell backwards. A bullet to the stomach mortally wounded Sheriff Culp. Constable Meadows expired instantly from a bullet to the brain.[10]

As Sheriff Culp lay dying, he watched Glass get to his feet and gather the reins of his horse, which had spooked in the gunfire. The lawman was confused. He was sure they had shot the outlaw and killed him. He watched Glass leap onto his ride and hurry off.

Information gleaned from the dying lawman by Captain Sixkiller, who arrived at the site less than an hour after the incident, disclosed that Glass wore a breastplate that deflected bullets. A posse was quickly organized and gave chase. Captain Sixkiller told the editor of the *Indian Journal* that it was going to be difficult to catch Glass because "he knows every inch of the country and has many friends who will hide him or fight for him as the case may require."[11]

Captain Sixkiller was well aware of Dick Glass's troubled past, the men who aligned themselves with him, and the crimes that made him so hated that he had to leave his home near Wagoner, less than one hundred miles from Muskogee. In July 1880 Glass had led a raid against some Cherokee Indians that he and his cohorts believed were keeping former slaves, some half black and Creek like Glass, from peacefully settling in the area. Two Creek Freedmen had been lynched by the Cherokee Nation for what Glass viewed as merely an attempt to "better their station in life." They were in fact stealing horses and, instead of letting the Creek Nation deal with punishing their own tribesmen as was the rule, Cherokee authorities had taken matters into their own hands.[12]

Glass and his followers decided to help themselves to the horses the Creek Freedmen were attempting to steal. In the process Glass shot and killed a Cherokee Indian named Billie Cobb and wounded another named Alex Norman. Both men were trying to stop Glass and his men from getting away with the animals. The incident caused a diplomatic crisis between the Creek and Cherokee Nations.

Glass and his ten-member gang fled the area and ended up in the neighborhood of Stonewall, Oklahoma Territory, where they entered the bootlegging business. Creek Lighthorsemen tracked Glass to the area and arrested him in September 1882. The outlaw was placed in jail in Winfield, Kansas, but quickly escaped and hurried back to Oklahoma Territory.[13] Three years later Glass was involved in another incident that caused trouble between full-blood and mixed-blood Creek Indians. Creek police officers were attempting to arrest a criminal associated with Glass. Glass and more than three hundred other freed slaves kept the force from apprehending the wanted man.[14] More Indian lawmen were dispatched to assist the other Lighthorsemen with their task, but Glass and his followers would not back down. US Army soldiers were called in to restore

order to the area. Once the troops had successfully quelled the disturbance, Glass drifted toward Muskogee with a band of fellow lawbreakers.

In October 1884 US marshals at Sacred Heart Mission in Asher,
Oklahoma Territory, received word from a rancher that Glass had been
spotted south of Tulsa with a herd of stolen livestock. For eleven months
Glass and his gang traveled back and forth from Texas to Kansas, stealing
horses and steers and selling bootleg liquor on a large scale. Glass and his
men always managed to elude authorities, frequently disappearing into
the Texas panhandle.[15]

By summer 1885 Glass was on his way to Oklahoma Territory again
with a new shipment of whiskey. Scouts that Captain Sixkiller had posted
at various spots along the banks of the Red River informed the lawman
that Glass's band was bringing more booze into the area, and that Glass
himself had been located in Dennison, Texas. Captain Sixkiller set out
with several other officers, including Charles LeFlore, to capture Glass
and his gang. The lawmen boarded a train at the last station on the Missouri Pacific Railroad and traveled north along the Red River toward
Texas.[16]

The officers located the desperados and their wagon just before
sunset on Friday, June 8, 1885. Without showing themselves the posse
passed around the outlaws' camp and hid in the timber on each side
of the road where the renegades would cross, then waited until morning. On Saturday morning Glass and his followers resumed their journey. He had armed men posted around the wagon in anticipation of
an ambush. Captain Sixkiller and the other officers waited until the
outlaws had relaxed their guard a bit, then leapt out onto the road-
way in front of them. The lawman ordered Glass to throw up his hands
and surrender.[17] Instead of obeying the command, each man went for
his gun and attempted to escape. According to the June 11, 1885, edition of the *Indian Journal,* "Glass pulled his pistol and turned to shoot
when a charge from Captain Sixkiller's shotgun went into his breast and

another into his head, killing him instantly. Jim Johnson (one of Glass's gang members) also attempted to shoot but a dose of lead settled him. In the meantime the wagon driver had whipped up, and he was going by. Two officers ordered him to halt. As he did they fired, and he fell into the wagon apparently dead."[18]

Captain Sixkiller pursued the outlaws trying to flee the scene. The driver of the wagon, who had only been slightly wounded, grabbed a Winchester belonging to Glass and the reins of the spooked team of horses, and urged them to a gallop away from the gunfire. After a five-mile chase the horses gave out and the captain's men apprehended the driver. Captain Sixkiller and the posse returned to the spot where Glass and Johnson lay dead. The surviving members of the gang were arrested and several barrels of whiskey seized.[19]

The prisoners and the two bodies were transported to Colbert, Oklahoma Territory, where Glass was identified beyond a doubt. Glass and the other deceased outlaws were buried in Colbert. The other prisoners were taken to Fort Smith, Arkansas, to stand trial. Because Captain Sixkiller was the one who killed Glass, he received the one thousand dollar reward offered by the federal government for the criminal—dead or alive He also received an additional five hundred dollar reward offered by Chief Dennis Wolfe Bushyhead. It was the maximum amount allowed by Cherokee law.[20]

Back in Muskogee, Sixkiller's superiors and staff congratulated the captain for "successfully dispatching the duties of his office." Although Sixkiller was pleased that Glass's operation was out of business, he knew there would be others to take the criminal's place.

The larceny case against a white settler and petty criminal named Jeff Bollen paled in comparison to Captain Sixkiller's dealings with Dick Glass, but he handled the matter with equal diligence. Bollen stole a prized mule from the home of a widow named Mrs. D. Trent and fled the area with the animal. According to a Western Union telegraph sent by the captain to law enforcement officials at Fort Smith, they were to apprehend Bollen should he reach Arkansas. A warrant was issued for Bollen's arrest, and Captain Sixkiller and his deputies set out in the direction the outlaw was last seen riding.[21]

The mule thief was captured at a makeshift camp thirty miles outside of Muskogee. Bollen was arrested without incident and held over for trial. The key witness against Bollen turned out to be his half brother, John, who told Captain Sixkiller that the mule was in a stable and Bollen had knocked the fence over to get to the animal. "I followed his tracks and the tracks of the mule about a mile to Mike Conden's place (a nearby ranch) where I noticed that a saddle was missing," John reported to the authorities. "The next morning I wound around the neighborhood to find if anybody had left the country. The tracks that led away from the Condens' place corresponded with the tracks I had seen the day before. I knew his tracks. He had a mismatched pair of boots—that is a pair of boots belonging to one foot and I recognized the tracks before I learned he (the mule) was missing. I think both boots were rights. The mule belonged to the woman keeping house for me at that time. I had her mule in my charge. It was a little black male or a very dark brown; seven years-old this spring, about fourteen hands high, not branded and worth $100. The saddle was worth $3 or $4."[22] John's compelling testimony helped convict Bollen of larceny. On August 18, 1885, he was sentenced to a year in jail.[23]

Whatever the severity of the offense committed by lawless characters on Indian land or government property, citizens in Muskogee were confident that Captain Sixkiller would do his job well. According to the memoirs of S. R. Lewis, a resident of the Cherokee Nation during the time the captain was on the job: "Captain Sixkiller was a man of great courage and rendered splendid service in enforcing the laws called upon to enforce."[24]

Sam's experience as a lawman taught him that minor offenders left unchallenged could go on to commit major crimes. Richard F. Vann, a

Chickasaw Indian better known as Dick Vann, was one such offender. Until mid-1884 most of Vann's transgressions consisted of stealing grain for his horses or disorderly conduct. The first mention of his misdeeds appeared in the April 12, 1883, edition of the *Indian Journal*. The newspaper reported that "during a visit with friends near Fort Gibson, Vann's pistol accidentally discharged striking a passerby on the wrist."[25] On May 22, 1884, Vann and his brother, Herman, were arrested for killing Matt Scales at Webbers Falls in eastern Oklahoma Territory.[26] The two men insisted they had nothing to do with Scales's murder and gave themselves up without a fight. The only evidence the authorities had against them was a statement from Scales just before he died. Since his character was considered questionable, the Vanns were released after a few days. Law enforcement officials eventually dismissed the accusation completely.

On October 9, 1884, Vann was watching a horse race in Muskogee when he decided to remove his pistol and lay it on the stands near him. After the event was over he left, absentmindedly leaving the gun behind. Two Lighthorsemen who saw him leave immediately took possession of the weapon. Quickly realizing his mistake, Vann returned for the gun just in time to see the police take it. When Vann confronted the lawmen, demanding his gun back, a number of his friends gathered around the Lighthorsemen and began to yell and scream at the policemen to return the gun. A crowd of concerned citizens armed with Winchesters and shotguns gathered to hear the harsh words exchanged between the Lighthorsemen and Vann. When it became clear to Vann and his cohorts that the citizens were ready to back up the police, the incident was resolved peacefully. Vann didn't stay out of trouble long. In December 1884 he was arrested for attempted murder.[27]

At the time, Dick Vann was a part-time bootlegger and full-time cattle rustler in the area of Fort Gibson in Muskogee County, Oklahoma Territory. On December 18, 1884, he threatened to kill a post trader named John Hammer. The intended victim initially reported the threat to the authorities at Fort Smith, Arkansas. Hammer told police there that while he was visiting a restaurant and hotel in Fort Gibson, Vann started calling him names and drew his pistol to show him he meant business. "He fired at me, but the gun misfired and I was unharmed," the post trader later recounted in a written statement. "I grabbed him and we fought over the gun. I don't know what was wrong with him." He ultimately retrieved the weapon from Vann and requested a deputy be sent to the area to take possession of the gun and arrest the assailant. "If you think there are any more witnesses needed, I can get more," Hammer added before concluding his statement.[28]

Law enforcement was dispatched to Fort Gibson, and Vann was taken into custody and made to stand trial. At the hearing Vann told the court that he was the victim and that he was only defending himself against an attack from Hammer. Four witnesses appeared at the trial ready to back up Vann's story: Milo Hoyt, his son Black Hoyt, Dave Andrews, and Westly Martin. Three of the men had previous run-ins with the law and had reputations for violence.

Milo Hoyt's troubles with the law had to do with his objection to paying taxes. He was a wealthy Cherokee Indian who had been adopted by the Choctaw Nation and owned several hundred acres of land. In early 1884 the Choctaw Nation passed a law that every white man living in the nation, or the employer of a white man living in the nation, was required to pay a heavy tax. Milo had several white men working for him and was outraged by the edict. He refused to pay, and authorities seized his livestock to settle the debt. Shortly thereafter the district courthouse at La Grange, Mississippi, was burned down, and Milo was the prime suspect. The Choctaw Lighthorsemen pursued Milo and his band of militants into the Cherokee Nation. Milo managed to elude the Cherokee police as well.[29]

Somewhere along the way Dick Vann fell in with Milo and his group. Milo didn't hesitate to come to Vann's defense when he was accused of trying to kill Hammer. Milo testified that Vann had both hands in the pockets of his overcoat and never produced a weapon. "I observed afterwards he had a self-cocking Smith and Wesson .38 caliber revolver in his right pocket, but kept it there," he told the court in February 1885. "The right pocket of the overcoat was much torn in the struggle between Hammer and Vann. That's the only time the pistol was seen by Hammer. I went to see Vann and asked him to give me his pistol, which at that time was in the clutches of both Hammer and Vann. In reply he said, 'I'm afraid Hammer will shoot me.' I replied, 'If he does, I'll shoot him.'"[30]

The jury did not believe Vann's account of the event or his witnesses. He was found guilty, but his lawyer asked the judge to set aside the verdict. He accused the jury of being biased against his client and supporters and argued that there wasn't sufficient evidence to convict Vann. The attorney's request was denied. Before a second trial could be held, Vann's lawyer appealed to a higher court and managed to get a pardon for his client.[31]

Once Vann was pardoned, he decided to leave the area and make his way to Muskogee where his sister and brother-in-law lived. His brother-in-law, Alf Cunningham, was a mixed-blood Cherokee Indian who harbored a long-standing resentment of the Lighthorsemen and lawmen in general. Newspaper reporters at the *Indian Journal* tried to uncover what had initially sparked Alf's animosity toward police as a whole, and Captain Sixkiller in particular. According to the August 19, 1880, edition of the *Indian Journal*, "We did not get all the particulars of the personal difficulties between Captain Sixkiller, of the Indian police, and Alf Cunningham. We think it began at the meat market (in Muskogee) Monday morning—but of this we were informed—that 'Alf' was knocked about some and his revolver taken from him by the officer. The weapon was discharged during the dispute while 'Alf' was trying to get in range to shoot."[32]

Vann became acquainted with Alf while he was courting Vann's sister. Apart from his battles with law enforcement, not much is known about

Cunningham. He had a way with horses, guitars, and guns and Vann admired him. Vann was looking forward to seeing Alf when he arrived in Muskogee, but he didn't arrive alone. Vann brought along two men who he thought would admire his brother-in-law as much as he did—Milo and Black Hoyt. Each would have an altercation with the territory's most renowned lawman, Captain Sixkiller. The result of their disagreements would be death.[33]

7

KEEPING THE PEACE

Captain Sixkiller did a good stroke of business this Sunday.
—COMMENT IN THE *INDIAN JOURNAL* NEWSPAPER
ABOUT THE JOB THE LAWMAN DID IN JUST ONE DAY,
DECEMBER 17, 1885

CAPTAIN SAM SIXKILLER CROSSED THE TIMBER-LINED BANKS OF THE Arkansas River atop a big, brown roan. The well-traveled trail that lay out in front of him looked like an ecru ribbon thrown down across the prairie grass. Riding a few paces behind the lawman was Deputy Bill Drew. Neither man spoke as they traveled. A herd of cattle in the near distance plodded along slowly toward a small stream. A couple of calves held back, bawling for their mothers, who had left them a safe distance behind. Upon reaching the stream the cows buried their noses in the water. They paid no attention to the approaching riders as they enjoyed a refreshing drink.[1]

Captain Sixkiller pulled back on the reins of his horse, slowing the animal's pace. He stared thoughtfully, considering the proximity of the cattle to the crude camp behind the field of prairie grass reaching to the horizon. Deputy Drew watched the captain, waiting for the officer to proceed. Both men knew the danger inherent in the job they'd set out to do that day in early January 1886. They were tracking a murderer named Alfred "Alf" Rushing, also known as Ed Brown.[2]

Nine years prior to Captain Sixkiller leaving Muskogee on a cold winter's day to apprehend Rushing, the elusive rowdy had shot and killed the marshal of Wortham, Texas.[3] The Houston and Texas Central Railway ran through this busy cotton farm community, attracting nefarious characters like Rushing, a cattle rustler and bootlegger who hoped to make a fortune selling liquor and robbing business owners in the farming town. On December 8, 1879, Rushing and two accomplices had ridden into Wortham and made their way to J. J. Stubb's general store. All three were armed with shotguns and hell-bent on retrieving a pistol they claimed Stubbs had stolen from them.[4]

It wasn't the first time Stubbs had been accused of stealing the pistol from Rushing. Although Stubbs denied taking the gun, the men continued to come around and harass him for the item. They refused to accept the storeowner's claim that he knew nothing of it. Rushing finally told him he intended to get seventeen dollars for the weapon before he left or there would be "hell to pay."[5]

The volatile display Rushing and his cohorts, Harv Scruggs and Frank Carter, made attracted the attention of Wortham's dutiful and dedicated city marshal, Jackson T. Barfield. According to the newspaper the *Galveston Daily News*, "Marshal Barfield quietly walked across the street (from the jail) to the store and asked the men in a friendly manner not to raise a disturbance and to be more quiet.[6]

"The marshal was not accused to his face of having taken the pistol, but seemed to be trying to pacify them and apprehend no danger to himself. Turning his back upon them to walk off, he was shot in the back by Alf Rushing with nine buckshot passing through his body and three through the heart.

"They had previously mounted their horses and immediately upon firing they wheeled and under a shower of buckshot, with their horses at full speed, left town. As quickly as possible several citizens procured horses and went in hot pursuit. Some distance from town they turned on their pursuers; several shots were exchanged and they continued their flight."[7]

Carter and his horse were slightly wounded in the encounter. The animal was limping, so he decided to abandon his ride and make a run for it. The hastily formed posse captured Carter hurrying across a field. Scruggs and Rushing escaped. Every attempt was made by Wortham citizens to locate the two outlaws, but to no avail. It was rumored that Rushing was hiding out in the area of Pin Oak Creek, more than eleven miles from Wortham, and that several friends and family members were protecting him from arrest. Rushing already had warrants out for his arrest for the murder of Marshal Barfield. Wanted posters for Rushing read: "$1,000 reward for the arrest and detention of Alfred Rushing, who on the 3rd of December 1877 murdered Jackson Barfield the marshal of Wortham, Texas. He is 6 ft. 2 inches high. Weighs between 160 and 175 lbs; hair, a dark sandy red, florid complexion, wolfish look, and is bold to reckless."[8]

In late 1885 Captain Sixkiller was informed by officials at the extradition service that a man fitting Rushing's description was living and working as a rancher near Webbers Falls in Muskogee County, Oklahoma Territory. Captain Sixkiller was determined to bring the criminal to justice.[9]

Captain Sixkiller and Deputy Drew rode slowly behind a large herd of steers, their faces numb from the cold and their breath visible in the frosty air. Smoke wafted from a chimney on a small cabin several miles ahead of them. The lawmen suspected Rushing was inside. Following his lead, Drew helped the captain separate twenty to thirty cows from the herd and push them toward the cabin. Using ropes hanging off the horns of their saddles, the men waved at the animals, urging them to move along. While they were still a distance from the cabin, a solitary man opened the front door and stood in the frame, watching. Captain Sixkiller and the deputy preceded cautiously, their guns at the ready.

As the captain and the deputy got closer to the cabin, they could see a dark, red-headed man in the door pick up a rifle beside him and hold it in his hands in front of his body. The two lawmen exchanged an apprehensive look. "Easy," Captain Sixkiller said to the deputy in a soft, low voice. The armed figure in the door maintained a close vigil on the two riders as they came near, driving the unmarked cattle in front of them.

Captain Sixkiller greeted the man with a nod of his head and a tired smile. He told the man that he and his partner were driving their herd to the station in Vinita and asked if he could put the animals in the empty corral in front of the building. The man studied the scene for a moment and agreed. He lowered his gun and introduced himself to the pair as Ed Brown. The captain recognized Rushing's alias but gave nothing away as he offered a "much obliged" and drove the cattle toward the pen. Deputy Drew followed along. Some of the cows protested loudly and balked at the pace of the move. Captain Sixkiller pretended the animals were too unruly for him and the deputy to handle and asked Rushing to give them a hand. Rushing seemed none too eager to leave the warmth of his cabin but, after a brief moment set his gun aside, grabbed his coat, and headed out the door.

The deputy rode to the gate on the corral and swung it open. Rushing stood to one side of the herd, waving his hat back and forth over the low-headed cows. Captain Sixkiller sat atop his horse hurrying the cattle along from the back. Rushing was so busy with the animals he didn't notice the captain ride up behind him and draw his gun. Rushing froze under the threat of the weapon. Captain Sixkiller announced that he was a US marshal and introduced Drew as his deputy. The outlaw offered no resistance.[10]

The January 28, 1886, edition of the Muskogee *Indian Journal* reported that Rushing "denied he is the man wanted by the officers." Captain Sixkiller was confident they had the right party.[11] The accused was held at the Muskogee jail until Texas officers came to get him. Rushing escaped before he was brought to trial and remained at large until 1930, when law enforcement officials learned he was living in Sweetwater, Texas. By then he was seventy-four years old and in poor health. He died of natural causes on December 12, 1930.[12]

With the exception of a short period of time between the fall of 1882 and February 1884, Captain Sixkiller had always returned home to his wife, Fannie, and their six children after searching for lawbreakers on the run. Fannie continued to struggle with consumption and, after 1880, with long bouts of depression over the loss of their daughter Minnie, born in 1871. Nine-year-old Minnie, using a plank for support, had paddled from the shallow section of a pond, where she had been swimming with friends, to the deep end. She lost her grip on the plank and sank into the deep water. Her body was recovered within a few minutes and every attempt was made to revive her, but it was too late—little Minnie had drowned.[13] Fannie grieved her demise tremendously.

Likely owing to the stress of Fannie's debilitating illness and the tension associated with spending long periods of time apart from his wife, Captain Sixkiller strayed from his marriage vows. His affair with Mary Malissia Murphey was brief. Their son, James Thomas Sixkiller, was born on February 11, 1874. Shortly after James arrived, Mary died from complications in childbirth. A young woman and her husband in a nearby town adopted the baby. By all accounts from his children, friends, and extended family, Captain Sixkiller was a devoted father and faithful provider. He made such an impact on his son Samuel Rasmus Sixkiller (with Fannie Foreman, born on February 13, 1877), that Samuel followed him into law enforcement.[14]

At forty-four years of age and with more than ten years' experience as an officer of the law, Captain Sixkiller was one of the most respected men in the field. Railroad officials, jailers, and judges referred to him as the "terror of outlaws." Chief Deputy J. M. Huffington of Fort Worth, Texas, who had worked with Captain Sixkiller on several occasions, called him "one of the best and bravest officers that ever rode the Indian

Country." US District Judge Isaac Parker declared Captain Sixkiller to be "an exceptional lawman—a man who knows no fear." Captain Sixkiller had helped rid Oklahoma Territory of many criminal operations, and no one was more grateful for that than the management of the Missouri-Kansas-Texas Railroad. Gangs began targeting the Katy shortly after it laid the first tracks in the Cherokee Nation. Train robbery was not a federal offense unless the US mail was stolen, which it was most of the time. As a US deputy marshal and agent for the railway, Captain Sixkiller was acting in a dual capacity when he tracked and arrested train robbers. During the time he was an agent, he captured fourteen particularly notorious train robbers, all of whom were hanged for their misdeeds.[15]

Although the Dalton brothers did not officially rob a train until 1892, the famous outlaws studied the Katy's operation in Vinita and Muskogee, including its schedule of stops. According to the January 17, 1901, edition of the *Tyrone Daily Herald* in Tyrone, Pennsylvania, Captain Sixkiller was certain death for the road agents. The Daltons were always "on the lookout for the lawman and kept their weapons at the ready at all times."[16]

All four Dalton boys were born in Missouri, but their family followed the homesteaders onto the Indian lands in Oklahoma Territory in 1882. At the beginning of the 1880s, pressure for good land became acute, and demand that the US government open part of the Indian Territory for settlement was irresistible. On April 22, 1889, a proclamation made by President Benjamin Harrison opened the territory to those who wanted to settle there. A group of federal scouts was on hand to hold the vast, eager crowd in check until the appointed time of noon, when they could cross into the area now known as Oklahoma and begin filing claims.[17]

Precisely at noon the signal was given, and the stampede of humanity was under way. On the first day almost ten thousand settlers joined the rush to pitch tents, stake out claims, and throw up shacks. Members of the Five Civilized Tribes feared that this action meant they would once again face dispossession and removal. Chiefs representing all the

Judge Isaac Parker, the "Hanging Judge," sentenced 160 men to the gallows during two decades of keeping a tight rein on Indian Territory. Parker called Captain Sixkiller the most dependable deputy marshall in Oklahoma Territory. COURTESY WESTERN HISTORY COLLECTIONS, UNIVERSITY OF OKLAHOMA LIBRARIES (ROSE 1750)

tribes called on the federal government to honor the treaty they had made with them, which noted that the government was obliged to protect the Indian Nations' borders, sovereignty, and land tenure. The government was slow to respond, and when it did the issue was not resolved in the Indians' favor.

The Daltons were among the thousands of white people that settled in the area. But they were not content to be legitimate farmers or ranchers. Before they got bold enough to steal from the railroad, they had been involved in large-scale stock rustling and whiskey sales.[18]

Captain Sixkiller and his men fought continually against bootleggers. Supplies of liquor were replenished as quickly as authorities seized the illegal product. In February 1885 Captain Sixkiller arrested several Cherokee boys for consuming and selling alcohol. The boys pled guilty and told the US deputy marshal where they got the whiskey. According to the August 16, 1885, edition of the *Muskogee Phoenix* newspaper: "White traders gave the alcohol to the youth and planned to take a percentage of whatever was made from the whiskey sold."[19] The alcohol was made in Arkansas and considered to be more potent than whiskey produced anywhere else. The newspaper article reported that "the drink (referred to as the Blind Tiger) was strong enough to kill anything but Indians."[20]

Retail liquor dealers ranging from Charles Hughes, a repeat offender in the Indian Territory, to Bluford Sixkiller, a relative of the captain's and the assistant chief of the Ketoowahs (a religious organization that preserves the culture and teaching of the Cherokee Nation), were charged with and tried for selling the whiskey to the Indians.

With few exceptions, apprehending a bootlegging suspect was a dangerous job for Muskogee authorities. Many offenders, such as a forty-year-old white man known only as "Wright," resisted arrest. Wright was a violent and brazen trader from northern Missouri. From the spring of 1861 to the summer of 1863, he had managed to sell whiskey to members of the Five Civilized Tribes without getting caught. Officers in

Savanna, a town in present-day Pittsburg County, Oklahoma, came the closest to capturing the criminal, but he managed to get away under a hail of gunfire.[21]

In mid-June 1883 Wright hauled a wagonload of whiskey into Eufaula, located in present-day McIntosh County, Oklahoma. Brazen and unafraid, he opened one of the barrels of liquor on the main street of the town and began serving eager customers without any interference. The bold venture was so profitable Wright decided to peddle his merchandise in another burg in the Oklahoma Territory, a place called Fishertown. When Captain Sixkiller heard the bootlegger was so flagrantly breaking the law, he decided to take him in.[22]

Captain Sixkiller's brother Henry accompanied him to the area, and the pair tracked Wright to the home of his accomplice, Tom Watson. Wright answered the door holding a shotgun in his hand. Captain Sixkiller and Henry slowly raised their hands in the air. Wright and Watson laughed uproariously. The lawmen and the outlaws exchanged a few words and then Wright glanced away for a moment. In that moment the captain quickly removed his pistol from its holster and leveled it at Wright's head. "Hands up," Captain Sixkiller ordered. Wright was stunned and didn't move for second or two, and then he suddenly cocked the hammer back on his gun. But he wasn't fast enough. Captain Sixkiller fired a split second ahead of the outlaw. Wright's gun went off in the air as he hit the ground, dead. Before Watson could process what had happened to his partner in crime, Captain Sixkiller pointed his pistol at him and shook his head. "You're next if you don't do as you're told," he warned Watson. The man nodded and put up his hands.[23]

Before Captain Sixkiller and Henry transported Watson and Wright back to Muskogee, they searched the property, but found only ten gallons of whiskey. Watson claimed Wright had brought more than one hundred gallons with him when he came to Eufaula, but that Wright had buried the liquor and Watson didn't know where. Wright left behind a fourteen-year-old wife at a makeshift ranch near Fishertown in the Indian Territory.

Captain Sixkiller's gritty, bulldog tenacity and ability to apprehend elusive criminals continually earned him respect among judges and politicians. George Washington Steele, the first Oklahoma Territorial Governor, considered the captain one of the most dependable deputy marshals in the United States. Lawbreakers, too, had a healthy respect for Captain Sixkiller, and many went to great pains to ensure he never got on their trail.[24]

Muskogee wasn't lacking in criminal activity. One particular incident that required Captain Sixkiller's grit and expertise occurred in mid-December 1885. A drunk, belligerent vagrant had stolen a pistol from a local bakery, and the owners of the eatery wanted the item back. The captain and brother Henry spotted the culprit, Tandy Walker, at the stable while they were tending to their horses. Neither of the lawmen was carrying his weapons, so they did not approach the inebriated thief. Henry followed Walker to the hotel where he was staying; Captain Sixkiller fetched their guns and met Henry at the hotel. The two strapped their holsters on and checked to make sure their pistols were loaded. Walker had staggered to his room, and the lawmen decided to take him there.[25]

According to a report of the incident in the *Indian Journal* newspaper, when the policemen stepped into the room, Walker was sitting on the bed and another drifter named Gambol was seated in a chair by the window. Their pistols and Winchesters were within easy reach. "Before they had time to stir they were looking into the muzzle of Captain Sixkiller's pistol and were ordered to 'throw up and move away from those arms.'"[26]

The men did as they were told and were then handcuffed and escorted to jail. The governor of the Choctaw Nation had offered a reward of six hundred dollars for the pair. Captain Sixkiller would turn over Walker and Gambol as soon as the reward was paid.[27]

Walker told Captain Sixkiller that "if they'd had half a chance they would have made a fight." Walker further commented that "he'd die before he goes to trial." He was wanted for the shooting death of a woman in the Choctaw Nation. Walker had been trying to kill a man named Sol Folsum. He fired his gun into Folsum's home late one night, but the bullet hit a woman sleeping in Folsum's bed and her little girl lying beside her. The woman died from gunshot wounds to the chest and the girl was seriously injured.[28]

8

DIFFICULTIES WITH DICK VANN

Captain Sixkiller is in town. I will say to those living in the Territory and who think of dying soon that Johnny Schuller has the cheapest and best coffins and caskets.

—AN ADVERTISER WHO ANTICIPATED AN INCREASE IN
BUSINESS NOW THAT THE CAPTAIN HAD RETURNED TO
MUSKOGEE, *INDIAN JOURNAL,* JANUARY 22, 1885

IT WAS A WARM SEPTEMBER EVENING IN 1886 WHEN THE CITIZENS OF Muskogee gathered in the center of town to enjoy a concert given by the Muskogee Amateur Italienne Musical Society. Horses and wagons lined the streets. The performers tuned their instruments and greeted crowd members anxious to express their support. Excited children chased one another around, and families jockeyed for the best positions in front of a crude bandstand. Women huddled together discussing their day and comforting fussy infants who were unsettled by the flurry of activity.[1]

Before the event officially began, the sound of rapid gunfire echoed off the buildings that framed the main thoroughfare. The gunshots grew louder, and suddenly a pair of horsemen appeared riding pell-mell toward the congregation. People scattered. Running for cover, families disappeared into businesses and homes. The cries of astonishment and fear from the unassuming townspeople had no effect on the two riders. Black Hoyt, a half-blood Cherokee with whom Captain Sixkiller had previous dealings, and a white man named Jess Nicholson gouged their boot spurs into the sides of their mounts and charged down the street, shooting their weapons at anything that moved.[2]

The out-of-control men were drunk and enjoying the chaos their wild behavior caused among the startled townspeople. Captain Sixkiller and the police officers that worked with him, including Charles LeFlore, rushed onto the scene brandishing their own guns. The captain shouted at Hoyt and Nicholson to stop, but the men were not inclined to do so. After a few moments of waiting for the two rowdies to do as they were told, the Muskogee police force managed to corner the riders. LeFlore ordered them to throw their pistols down, and Captain Sixkiller informed them they were under arrest. Neither of the men complied.[3]

A tense hush filled the air as Hoyt and Nicholson considered their options. The captain studied the belligerent looks on their darkly flushed features. "Give us your guns now," he demanded, "before someone gets hurt." Hoyt shifted in his saddle and rubbed off the sweat standing on his chin with his right shoulder. His arm was missing from the elbow down, and his shirtsleeve was pinned over the remaining portion of the limb. Hoyt had lost his arm in June 1886 after he was shot by an unknown assailant while at Fort Gibson, Oklahoma Territory. The bullet fractured the lower third of the appendage, and amputation was his only chance of recovery. Hoyt and his father, Milo, objected at first, but after conferring with a second doctor, realized there was no other option. The younger Hoyt recovered quickly from the chloroform and, as soon as he could, left the post doctor's office to avoid any further attempts on his life. With Milo's help he learned how to ride and shoot holding the reins of his horse and pistol in the same hand.[4]

Hoyt smiled a nervous smile and shifted his glance back and forth from Charles LeFlore to Captain Sixkiller. The captain wore a serious, determined expression. Hoyt screwed up all his drunken courage and nodded. "Go to hell!" he barked at the lawmen.[5]

Almost simultaneously Hoyt and Captain Sixkiller drew their weapons. The men on either side of the two did the same. Shots rang out thick and fast. When the smoke cleared, Nicholson had been hit in the heel of his foot, and a bullet had grazed Captain Sixkiller's arm. Nicholson was bleeding badly when he whipped his horse around and raced away from the chaos. One of the officers gave chase. Hoyt was too dazed from the incident and liquor to attempt a getaway. The captain arrested him and led him to jail. Nicholson managed to elude the police, but given the serious nature of his wound, none of the lawmen believed he would get far.[6]

With the exception of Black Hoyt's father, Milo, most Muskogee residents were pleased that Black had been apprehended. Milo Hoyt had a long, volatile history with Captain Sixkiller and other members of the Lighthorsemen. In 1882 Milo had been involved in a fray southeast of Eufaula in Oklahoma Territory. A horse race in the elder Hoyt's neighborhood had been planned, but the owners of the horses and some of the spectators got into an argument over the length of the race and the number of entries allowed, so the event was canceled before it began.

According to the October 12, 1882, edition of the *Indian Journal,* a number of men on hand to watch the race retired to Hoyt's barn to gamble and drink. "John Post, a worthless but not a quarrelsome mulatto," the article read, "had been playing in the game of poker, but became boisterous and was not allowed to participate any longer and was finally kicked out of the barn." Post was insulted and angry by the treatment and returned with a knife. He advanced on Hoyt, who stepped back a few paces, drew his gun, and fired. The bullet entered one of Post's lungs and exited near the spine. He died three days later from the wound. Hoyt successfully pleaded self-defense.[7]

In another incident in 1884, Milo Hoyt had been accused of "violating the laws of the Choctaw Nation and defying, by armed resistance, her constituted authorities." Milo resented anyone who interfered with his illegal activities, which consisted of theft and the buying and selling of whiskey. When Milo organized an outlaw militia in July 1884 to stand between law enforcement and his criminal behavior, Greenwood McCurtain, the governor of the Choctaw Nation, tried to suppress the miscreant's actions. Milo vowed to kill the governor and anyone else who stood in his way. Milo's son Black was just as misguided and duplicitous as his father.[8]

Captain Sixkiller was aware of Milo's background and fully expected that he would cause trouble when he learned Black had been locked up. Indeed, the morning after the gunfight with Nicholson and the younger Hoyt, Milo charged into Captain Sixkiller's office demanding his son be released. When the captain refused, Milo became combative and promised to kill the lawman if he didn't do as he was told. He was promptly arrested and charged with riotous conduct, carrying a dangerous weapon, and threatening a policeman.

While both Hoyts sat in jail, Muskogee law enforcement officials combed the countryside for Jess Nicholson. After a few days of searching, Captain Sixkiller learned that the fugitive was hiding at his friend Dick Vann's house. On September 14 the captain sent Lighthorsemen Bud Kell and Robert Sixton to arrest and bring him in. Given the fact that Nicholson was wounded, Captain Sixkiller believed he would surrender peacefully. Vann, however, had no intention of letting Nicholson be turned over to the law without a fight.

The sun had just set and the moon was rising high in the sky when Bud Kell and Robert Sixton reached Vann's place. "We got off our horses and started for the porch," Kell later recalled. "Vann came down and met us a little ways from the house. 'How you doing, Dick?' I asked. He had been drinking, but he answered me and we went on to the porch. I told him what we were after and Deputy Sixton told Mrs. Nicholson, who had come to the door at the same time. She commenced screaming, then slammed the door. Sixton stepped toward the door and Vann said, 'By God, you cannot take Jesse away. You'll have to kill me or I'll kill you.' He waved his pistol over his head as he said this and then rested the gun at his thigh, pointing it at Deputy Sixton. I then showed him the warrant for Nicholson's arrest. 'He's bad off,' Vann bit back. 'You bastards shot him.'" Bud assured Vann that Nicholson would be treated for his injury, but Vann was not satisfied. He leveled his gun at the policeman and pulled the hammer back. "'Get out of here before I kill you,' he hissed. The officer tried to reason with him, but Vann refused to back down. The lawman departed, promising to return with reinforcements. 'We'll be back for Nicholson and you,' he warned."[9]

Captain Sixkiller was more annoyed than surprised to learn how Vann had reacted, given his previous encounter with the law in the winter of 1884, when he had shot a post trader and was subsequently pardoned for the crime. "He's pushing his good fortune," the captain told the officer who confronted Vann regarding Nicholson. "I'd think he wouldn't want any more trouble with the law. But, if that is what he wants, we'll have a warrant made out for obstructing an officer in performance of his duty."[10]

While Captain Sixkiller filled out the paperwork necessary to jail Vann, Jess Nicholson slowly bled to death. Vann was incensed over his friend's demise and blamed Sixkiller for what he believed was an abuse of power. He was committed to making the lawman pay for Nicholson's death. Milo Hoyt, who was released from jail on September 17, 1886, without his son, was in complete agreement with Vann.

Milo wanted the captain dead, but wasn't willing to stay in Muskogee long enough to challenge the lawman. As soon as his son was set free, Milo escorted him to Fort Smith. Black was under bond to appear in court there for the charge of impersonating a US police officer. Several months prior to the confrontation with Captain Sixkiller and his deputies on the streets of Muskogee, Black had boarded a train at Vinita with a friend. To avoid purchasing a ticket, Black told the conductor he was a deputy marshal and the man traveling with him was his prisoner. The ticket taker told him he didn't have orders to transport any lawmen and didn't have the authority to approve such a thing without word from his superiors. He told the two men they had to pay to ride. Black paid for his friend, but wouldn't pay for himself. He was arrested before the train left the station.[11]

The warrant issued for Vann's arrest noted that he had opposed all officers of the United States. When the deputies returned to serve Vann with the papers, he surrendered without incident. He was held on five hundred dollars bail, and his case was set to be heard in court in November. Vann stood trial for his actions on November 6, 1886. The proceedings were short; he was found not guilty and released with time served. He was angry and insulted by the way he and Nicholson had been treated by the courts and Captain Sixkiller. He went to Alf Cunningham's home, and the two commiserated over how they'd been treated by the law. The two swore vengeance.[12]

Any hope Vann had that Black might return to help him do away with Captain Sixkiller died when he learned a grand jury had indicted Black on the charge of impersonating a US officer. Milo Hoyt and his men weren't available to lend a hand either. Milo disbanded his militia and, left unprotected, was shot and killed by an unknown assailant. Not long before his death, Milo had sent word to the editor of the *Indian Journal* that he had no desire to ever return to the Choctaw Nation: "Though he is perfectly willing to pay all fines assessed against him, but as far as going there to live, no money could hire him to."[13]

Dick Vann managed to recruit other brooding renegades to his group—men with their own axes to grind with law enforcement in Muskogee and elsewhere. All were united in their belief that Captain Sixkiller should answer for what happened to Nicholson and the Hoyts. Vann had never had any trouble persuading men to join him in his illegal endeavors. In the summer of 1878, he had enlisted the help of several Cherokee Indians to terrorize a crowd of fairgoers in Muskogee. It was the first fair ever held in the town, and initially attendees were too busy enjoying the various exhibits and amusements to notice Vann and his friends racing their horses into the congested midway. Frantic people jumped out of the way and took cover as Vann and the other riders fired their revolvers over their heads, shooting out every light that was visible.[14]

Later that same evening Vann led his group on another shooting spree at the train depot. The Cherokee's Chief Dennis Wolfe Bushyhead and the editor of the *Oklahoma Star Newspaper* had been asleep in their berths when bullets tore through the windows and walls of the train. They both crawled out of their bunks and lay flat on the floor until the shooting stopped. Dick Vann and his party shot out the lights in two Missouri-Kansas-Texas Railroad cabooses and wounded a man asleep in the section house. The renegades were in town all the next day, but police officers did not attempt to arrest them, as they were well aware it might mean several dead men and a stampede from the fair.[15]

In 1883 Vann and Alf Cunningham had caused the same type of senseless disturbance in Tucson, Arizona Territory, terrorizing shoppers at a street market there. When the pair returned to the Indian Nation a few months later, they were involved in killing a man named Matt Scales near Webbers Falls, located in present-day Muskogee County, Oklahoma.[16]

While Vann was plotting his revenge against Captain Sixkiller, rumors that horse thieves had killed some lawmen were circulating throughout the territory. Since early October 1886 the captain had been transporting prisoners from Muskogee to Fort Smith. By mid-November, news of Sixkiller's passing was being telegraphed all over the country. Friends, family, and co-workers didn't learn the information was false until he arrived back, alive, at the town jail. Captain Sixkiller's demise proved to be untrue, but so was the report in the *Indian Journal* that claimed he "rode into Muskogee healthier and fatter than ever." In reality the lawman had taken ill while he was at Fort Smith and had not fully recovered. He was unable to shake whatever ailed him, even after taking a few days off from work to rest. In early December 1886 the captain and his wife decided a change of scenery might help him recuperate more quickly. They went to Vinita for a few days, returning on December 15, 1886. Captain Sixkiller was still not completely well when he returned to work, but he refused to take any more time from the job until Christmas.[17]

Several Muskogee residents planned to celebrate the holiday by attending a series of horse races to be held in town. It did not escape the captain's attention that a number of disreputable characters had arrived from various parts of the Indian Nation in anticipation of the event. Horse races in general attracted considerable attention and numerous bets changed hands, bootleg alcohol flowed freely, and occasional fights broke out. The *Indian Journal* noted in the December 22, 1886, edition of the paper that Captain Sixkiller and his officers promised to do their best to keep the streets safe for people during the time of the racing event. The *Indian Journal* added that citizens were happy the captain was feeling better and were confident that "he will soon be in his usual good health."[18]

Dick Vann, Alf Cunningham, and the renegades they consorted with had been out of town but planned to return for the holiday races. They would be on the lookout for anyone who stood between them and having a good time—especially Captain Sixkiller.[19]

9

A Terrible Tragedy

No one imagined that Muskogee was to lose a good citizen and the Territory one of the bravest of officers.
—*Indian Journal*, December 29, 1886

IN THE HOURS LEADING UP TO CHRISTMAS DAY 1886, MUSKOGEE WAS crowded with trail hands, farmers, drifters, and families. Mothers with their children in hand filtered in and out of the various stores that lined Main Street. Upon exiting the businesses, they would stop to admire the few displays in the windows. Most of the people visiting the mercantile, restaurants, and hotels on December 23 and 24 were primarily interested in horse racing. They hurried back and forth from the two-mile-long stretch of track outside town carrying food, alcohol, and cash. Men recklessly laid their money out on long-legged, sleepy-eyed geldings, some with US Army brands on their rumps. Spectators stood on either side of the unmarked track, anxiously waiting for the races to begin. Horses and riders lined up for the "dropped flag" start. The shouts and cheers from the onlookers nearly drowned out the sound of the animals' pounding hooves hurrying toward the finishing mark.[1]

Dick Vann was among the enthusiastic group enjoying the festivities. Whenever the horse he bet on won, he would celebrate with a round of thunderous applause and a long swig from a half-empty bottle of whiskey.

Alf Cunningham had had his share of drinks during the event too, and he and Dick took turns slapping one another on the back each time their wager paid off and laughing uproariously at their good fortune.

By early afternoon on Christmas Eve, both men were well on their way to getting drunk. They were belligerent with anyone jockeying for a better position to see the races than they had and were not immune from spitting in the face of people who celebrated a win when they lost. Vann finished off his bottle of whiskey and persuaded Cunningham to return to a place in town that would sell them more bootleg alcohol. Heavy gray clouds hung over the busy hamlet. A great V-shaped mass of ducks and Canada geese flying south passed overhead of the two as they walked away from the racetrack. The whole sky was filled with the soft whir of wings. Cunningham removed a gun tucked inside his coat pocket, pointed it at the birds, and pretended to shoot. Amused with himself, Cunningham laughed at his playful antics. Vann was too distracted by the sight of Tom Kennard, a Creek Lighthorseman, to do more than grin.[2]

Kennard stood in the doorway of the Commercial Hotel surveying the plethora of activity around him. Vann watched the officer carefully, then crossed to the other side of the street to avoid coming in contact with him. Unaware that anything was out of the ordinary at first, Cunningham followed his brother-in-law. When he spotted Kennard, he slowed down. Deciding against continuing on with Vann, he crossed the street and approached the lawman. Cunningham wore a contemptuous look as he approached Kennard. The bitterness he had for the law intensified as he drew closer to the Lighthorseman. Kennard, a descendant of black slaves once owned by the Creek Indians, saw Cunningham walking toward him but did not anticipate any trouble.[3]

Without hesitating, Cunningham jerked his gun out and pointed it at the lawman's face. He swore angrily at Kennard and threatened to kill him. Neither calm reasoning nor the promise of jail could persuade Cunningham to lower his weapon. A passerby, Mrs. Renfoe (wife of the town butcher), witnessed the exchange and grabbed the pistol. Before Cunningham was able to wrench it free, Kennard drew his own gun. He brought the butt of the weapon down hard on his cursing assailant's head, and Cunningham collapsed at his feet. Kennard took the gun away from him and left him where he fell.

Cunningham came to a few hours later. In the near distance he could hear whistling, hand clapping, and the sound of horses' hooves galloping down the racetrack. The crowd that had congregated in town to celebrate the season had thinned considerably. No one around seemed the slightest bit concerned that Cunningham was face down in the dirt. People cut a wide swatch around him to avoid any contact with the known trouble-maker. After inspecting the lump on his skull, he got to his feet. He was rattled but not enough to go home. He dusted off his clothes and then proceeded in the direction of the track.[4]

As the stillness of a starry night crept over Muskogee, Vann and Cunningham were seen together again wandering in and out of busi-nesses in the process of closing. Cunningham had relayed the tale of his encounter with Kennard to Vann, and both men were infuriated with the officer and every other Lighthorsemen in the Indian Nation. The memory of what happened to Jess Nicholson and Black Hoyt was still fresh in their minds. The men needed guns to do what they felt needed to be done. They tried to purchase a pistol from Turner & Byrnes' Hard-ware but were turned away by the owner of the store, C. F. Byrnes. Undeterred, they walked to the popular Mitchell House and went inside. Ray Farmer, the owner of the hotel, was too preoccupied with customers to notice the two enter and didn't see Cunningham steal his shotgun. The two left the establishment determined to use the weapon they had acquired.[5]

City Marshal Shelley Keyes was making his appointed rounds when Vann and Cunningham swaggered out of the Mitchell House in front of him. Cunningham raised the shotgun he was carrying to Keyes's face. The lawman instinctively held up his hands. Vann eyed the pistol on Keyes's hip and, before the officer had a chance to object, jerked it out of his holster. They left Keyes with his arms in the air and a bewildered look plastered across his face. Keyes watched them disappear into the alleyways and dark corners of the buildings.

Drunk on the courage the guns gave them, Vann and Cunningham scanned the vicinity for Lighthorseman Kennard. One of Muskogee's most well-known citizens, Armistead Cox, noticed the two men walking down the street and caught a glimpse of the weapons they were toting as they passed by an eatery called King's Restaurant. Cox wasn't completely sure, but he thought he saw the butt of the shotgun tucked under Cunningham's arm with the barrel pointed downward. The men continued on their way, and there was no chance for a second look.[6]

Captain Sixkiller was purchasing medicine at Dr. M. F. William's drugstore when Vann and Cunningham arrived on the scene. The lawman wasn't on duty; he had plans to take his family to a service at the Methodist Church, but first he had to get rid of the headache he was suffering from. He had been sick for one reason or another since late November after returning home from a trip to Fort Smith. In early December he and Fannie had traveled to Vinita to visit family. The hope was that his health would be restored during that time, but they were forced to come home on December 15 because the captain wasn't getting any better.[7]

As Captain Sixkiller stepped into the street, he saw the shadowy image of the armed men. They were silhouetted against the light from the hotel and butcher shop across the street. The captain was unarmed and had no reason to believe Vann and Cunningham were carrying weapons.

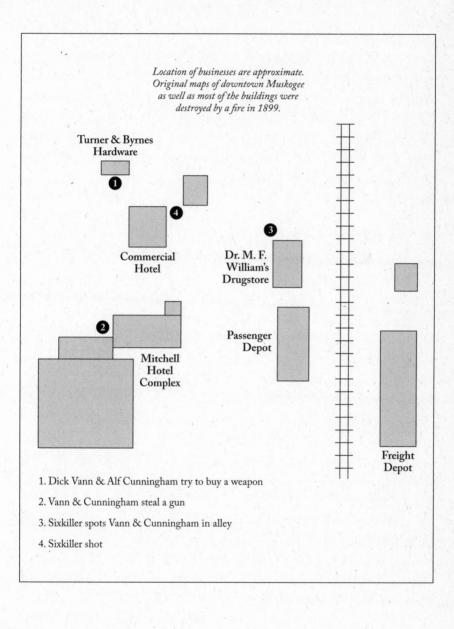

*Location of businesses are approximate.
Original maps of downtown Muskogee
as well as most of the buildings were
destroyed by a fire in 1899.*

Turner & Byrnes
Hardware

Commercial
Hotel

Dr. M. F.
William's
Drugstore

Mitchell
Hotel
Complex

Passenger
Depot

Freight
Depot

1. Dick Vann & Alf Cunningham try to buy a weapon

2. Vann & Cunningham steal a gun

3. Sixkiller spots Vann & Cunningham in alley

4. Sixkiller shot

He wasn't intimidated in the least. As he walked toward the pair, one of them called out his name. Vann then shouted, "You'd never do that to me again." Suddenly Cunningham fired the shotgun at the officer. Captain Sixkiller sprang forward before the full force of the shotgun shell made contact. He knocked the gun out of Cunningham's hands and fell to the ground. A few pellets had riddled his clothing, but none had penetrated the skin. Before the lawman could defend himself, Vann drew his pistol and fired four times. Blood oozed from the lawman's chest and head. All four bullets had met their target.

Captain Sixkiller struggled to get to his feet, staggered a bit, then dropped to his hands and knees. Vann pulled the hammer back on the gun again and shot him one more time. The lawman groaned as the fatal wound fought against every working internal organ. The captain winced in pain as he exhaled. One of the murderers leaned over his body as he breathed his last breath; when it was over the shooters fled.[8]

Rancher H. B. Spaulding and Armistead Cox were the first to arrive at the scene of the crime, followed by a gentleman named Nip Blackstone and the butcher, Jim Renfro. Cox checked to see if Captain Sixkiller was still alive. He knew by looking at his injured skull that it wasn't possible, but he had to be sure. It was a gruesome sight. The lawman had a hole in his face under his left cheekbone, and the skin was covered with powder burns from being shot at close range. The clothing around his waist was saturated with blood, and two bullets were lodged in his abdomen.[9]

City Marshal Keyes watched the men surround the deceased captain from across the street. He was overcome with guilt for letting the renegades get the best of him and take his gun. In an effort to conceal his identity from Vann and Cunningham, and anyone else who might have witnessed the exchange, he had turned his coat inside out and removed his hat. A reporter for the *Cherokee Advocate* who spotted Keyes noted:

"It seemed as though he might like to contract for a cast iron suit of clothes."[10]

Captain Sixkiller's lifeless frame was transported to the undertaker's office, where his body was prepared for burial. His wife, Fannie, and his children learned of the shocking news from the men who handled the lawman's remains. Fannie was inconsolable. Captain Sixkiller's killing was a hard truth for the community to accept as well. The loss was immediately felt throughout the entire Indian Nation. Recognizing the captain as the "head and heart of the Indian police," the public demanded swift justice.[11]

On Saturday morning, December 26, writs were issued for the killers and given to four US marshals: Frank Dalton, Tyson Greenbury, James Campbell, and H. J. Hayes. The writs read: "Dick Vann and Alf Cunningham feloniously, willfully, and premeditatedly, and with malice and forethought, killed and murdered Samuel Sixkiller, a Cherokee Indian."[12] For twenty-four hours the marshals searched vigorously for the murderers but could not locate them. An additional search took place on Monday, December 28, 1886. Captain Sixkiller's brothers Martin and Luke joined the posse along with three other members of the Lighthorsemen. The men decided to look for the runaway killers in the thick bottoms of Gooseneck Bend, ten miles east of Muskogee. It was the area Vann had traveled to in 1884 when he tried to escape justice for the attempted murder of John Hammer.[13]

The December 29, 1886, edition of the *Indian Journal* newspaper reported that after Vann and Cunningham had killed the captain, "they ran half leisurely down Main Street, turned the corner and passed the billiard hall as they headed out of town. Saturday night it was noted they attempted to lodge with an acquaintance named John Lowery who objected to them staying with him. Vann tried to change his mind by showing him the pistol he had and in the process the weapon discharged accidentally, the bullet going across the end of his thumb."[14]

While the police continued their search for the killers, several letters of condolence were sent to Captain Sixkiller's widow and his family. One of the letters Fannie received was from an executive of the Missouri Pacific Railway, Thomas Furlong. "Dear Madam: I was deeply pained to learn from this morning's paper of the sad calamity that had befallen you in the untimely and cruel death of your late husband. My wife and family desire with me to tender you our sincere sympathy in your terrible affliction." In addition to the letter, Furlong forwarded a resolution adopted by the railroad secret service to express the rail line's sentiment relative to Captain Sixkiller's tragic death.[15]

Whereas, by the hands of murderous assassins our esteemed friend Captain Sam Sixkiller has been taken from our midst, and while submitting to the all-wise and inscrutable Providence, we desire to express our sentiments, respecting this to us an irreparable loss of a tried and true friend, and to the United States Government a brave, honest and competent officer. Therefore, we, the members of the Missouri-Pacific Railway Secret Service Department at St. Louis assembled, deeply deplore the cruel and untimely death of our esteemed friend, Captain Sam Sixkiller, who endeared himself to the members of this department by his uniform kindness and invaluable assistance rendered us in the discharge of our duties, and while our grief in itself is great at the loss of our esteemed friend, we realize that the loss of such an exemplary husband and father is immeasurable, and therefore we desire to convey to his family our heartfelt sympathy in this their greatest hour of affliction.[16]

More than two thousand mourners attended Captain Sixkiller's funeral the Sunday after he was killed. The services were conducted at the Methodist Church and the eulogy delivered by Cherokee leaders from

Tahlequah. The church could not contain the friends that gathered to pay their respects. According to the December 29, 1886, edition of the *Indian Journal*, "People from nearly every part of the eastern portion of the territory attended the last rites."

Newspaper editors throughout the Indian Nation praised Captain Sixkiller for his heroism and courage. An editor for the *Indian Chieftain* in Vinita wrote that "a man with so little thought of danger should fall by violence seemed in no way strange." The *Indian Journal* editor noted: "The Captain has done probably more than any one person to free the railroad towns of this Territory of their dangerous and reckless elements, and to him the country owes a great degree the comparative security to life and property that it now enjoys." In a report made to the Commissioner of Indian Affairs in Washington, DC, Indian agent Robert L. Owens commended Captain Sixkiller, noting: "He died a martyr to the cause of law and order and had the respect and confidence of all the decent people in the country particularly of men like Honorable Isaac C. Parker, US Judge of this district."[17]

The procession that accompanied Captain Sixkiller's remains to the cemetery was staggering and a testimony to how much people thought of him. The crowd on hand at the graveyard was one of the largest ever assembled in that part of the country.[18]

The men responsible for the death of the revered Captain Sixkiller were two of the most wanted men in the Indian Nation. A fifteen hundred dollar reward was offered for their arrest. Friends of both Dick Vann and Alf Cunningham made it known that the men had every intention of turning themselves in to authorities and added that the pair were willing to stand trial, even though they believed Captain Sixkiller's associates would distort the facts in their case and make sure they were prosecuted to the bitter end. Vann and Cunningham wanted to wait ten days before surrendering themselves to the law. The nearly two-week span of time was to ensure that tempers had cooled and the public was ready to hear their side of the incident. Numerous officers were on the trail of Vann and Cunningham and were convinced they would apprehend the pair before the ten days ended.[19]

Vann and Cunningham were charged with the crime of murder by a Creek Indian court. When or if they were caught, they were to be turned over to Creek authorities. According to the compact existing between the Creek and Cherokee Nations, the Creek Nation had jurisdiction over the case. If Vann and Cunningham were arrested in the Cherokee Nation, they would have to be extradited to the Creek Nation to stand trial. Judge Parker wanted to help bring the fugitives to justice, but because all the parties involved in the murder were Cherokee, the federal court had no jurisdiction in the matter.[20]

After carefully considering the specifics of the case, the judge determined the only way the federal government could assist in arresting Alf Cunningham was to go after him for theft. The gun he had taken from the owner of the Mitchell House qualified as stealing, a crime well within Judge Parker's right to handle. He issued a writ giving his deputy marshals the authority to arrest Cunningham on a larceny charge. The murder charge took precedence over the crime of stealing. If the deputy marshals managed to apprehend Cunningham, they would turn him over to the proper court.[21]

While the hunt for the captain's assassins was in progress, another man was named to the slain lawman's post. William Fields, a US marshal and the former city marshal of Tahlequah, was Captain Sixkiller's successor. He was an accomplished officer who knew filling the vacancy left by his beloved predecessor would be a daunting task.[22] Several months after the death of Captain Sixkiller, newspapers were still praising his work. "There never was before and there never was afterwards an officer like Captain Sam Sixkiller," the February 24, 1887, edition of the

Muskogee Phoenix reported. "He was as handsome as an Apollo Belvedere; if there is a race born without fear, Sixkiller belonged to it. He had a figure like Mars divestible of immortality. It was worth a hundred miles' travel to see Sixkiller seated in his saddle, straight as Tecumseh: perhaps no man ever had a more complete mastery over a horse than the gallant captain."[23]

Captain Sixkiller's widow and children struggled with the loss of their loved one. Two of his brothers joined in the quest to track down his killers, and his sisters, sons, and daughters helped comfort their mother and care for the family home. Fannie died of consumption less than two years after her husband passed away. The obituary that ran in the July 11, 1889, edition of the *Muskogee Phoenix* recounted how she lived out her last days:

Mrs. Sixkiller had been quite ill for several months and it became apparent quite a time since that death was gradually approaching. Everything that loving friends and family could do for her comfort and ease was done with willing hands and after her death, sweetly resigned to an inevitable fate, trusting implicitly in the promise of her redeeming Savior, and while to us the fact that she must need be taken from her children, and they by her death became orphans, and that with one daughter prostrated upon a bed of sickness, seems doubly severe affliction, yet it was God's will, and His way is the right way, however shrouded in inexplicable mystery it may seem to us, and it is but our duty and privilege to calmly yield to His mandates however poignant with grief may seem the affliction, which is His Divine mercy and grace He seems fit to lay upon us.

Fannie leaves six children and hosts of relatives and friends, many of whom had known her for years, and all of whom testify to her excellent Christian character, loving and kind disposition.

She mourned the murder of her husband until her last breath was taken.[24]

A note on a picture of the captain hanging on the wall of Fannie and Sam's home reminded relatives how the lawman was abruptly taken from them: "Captain Sixkiller was gunned down in Muskogee by Alf Cunningham and Dick Vann."[25]

10

CHASING ASSASSINS

At present, preparations are underway for an active hunt to track down the men who shot an unarmed lawman.
—*INDIAN JOURNAL*, DECEMBER 29, 1886

BLACK HOYT WAS CAUGHT COMPLETELY BY SURPRISE WHEN A POSSE headed by Deputy Marshal Bud Kell charged into Hoyt's billiard hall in Muskogee on January 11, 1887, and leveled their weapons at him. Before Hoyt could fully appreciate the dilemma, Marshal Kell warned the one-armed outlaw to put his hand in the air or be killed where he stood. The felon stared stubbornly at the officers, and for a moment he was clearly intent on a gun battle. He wanted to draw the six-shooter on his hip, but the number of lawmen bearing down on him gave him pause. Finally, the posse received an answer to their ultimatum. Hoyt lifted his hand and he was quickly disarmed.[1]

The authorities explained to Hoyt that he was being arrested because his bond had been revoked. The two bondsmen who had pledged money and property as bail for his appearance in court could no longer provide such assurances. Hoyt's father, Milo Hoyt, who was the first of the two bondsmen, had been killed since his initial arrest in the fall of 1886. The second, Dick Vann, was on the run from the law.[2]

Hoyt was furious about being rearrested. He accused Marshal Kell of taking him into custody again because the lawman believed he knew where Vann was hiding. He was correct. He refused to help lead the officers to the fugitive and was promptly escorted to jail, where a new bond was made. His friends Frank Smith, Jim Lowrey, and Charley Vann (Dick's brother) put up the money to bond Hoyt out of jail.[3]

In late April 1887 authorities tracked Alf Cunningham to Stilwell, Oklahoma Territory, where he was captured at the home of a landowner named Perry Brewer. As the federal government had no authority to take Cunningham in for the murder of Captain Sixkiller, he was held on a larceny charge. According to the April 28, 1887, issue of the *Indian Chieftain* newspaper, Cunningham's arrest was a complicated matter and a source of some discord between the US court system and the leaders of the Indian Nation. "Alf Cunningham . . . is now in the Fort Smith jail," the article began, "that clause of the treaty placing the district where the crime of theft occurred within the jurisdiction of the federal court is, we understand, the authority under which the United States court writ was issued." Numerous letters were exchanged between the chiefs of the Creek and Cherokee Nations and Judge Isaac Parker at Fort Smith, Arkansas. Chiefs Legus Perryman and Dennis Wolfe Bushyhead requested Cunningham be extradited back to Oklahoma Territory to stand trial for the murder of Captain Sixkiller. The legal process to approve Cunningham's transfer from federal custody to the Indian Nation's jurisdiction would prove to be very slow.[4]

Meanwhile, Dick Vann was still on the loose. Lighthorsemen and local members of law enforcement combed the hills and plains from Vinita to Tahlequah. The streets of Muskogee were so overrun with officers that residents there said it reminded them of the days of the Civil War. The reason for such a presence of police in the town was the rumor that Dick Vann intended to pass through. He had made it known that his trip would be marked by violence. "This is not a friendly call," he stressed to his informant. Thirty to forty armed men patrolled Muskogee waiting for Vann to carry out his threat. He never arrived.[5]

Vann eluded the posse sent to track him down for the captain's murder and took cover around Fort Gibson, not far from Muskogee. As he had lived the life of a transient horse trader and whiskey smuggler who roamed around the Indian country at will, he knew where a person could best hide out. He had several friends who would keep his location secret as well. In mid-June 1887 he committed a crime among those faithful confidants, and his secure circumstances changed.[6] Once the wrongdoing was reported to police, a warrant was issued for Vann's arrest for the "heinous and hellish crime of rape." The June 23, 1887, edition of the *Indian Journal* reported the person Vann assaulted was a married lady living near the fort, whose husband was a soldier away on duty. "An organized pursuit and search is now being made for him," the short article continued. "We give the report for what it's worth, but one thing is positive, there was evidence enough presented to justify the issuance of the writ."[7]

Assassin Dick Vann fled from justice in the Fort Gibson, Oklahoma, area.
AUTHOR'S COLLECTION

While the Lighthorsemen were tracking Dick Vann and various courts were debating where Alf Cunningham would be tried first, politicians in Washington were discussing how best to safeguard Indian law-enforcement agents. Prompted by the cold-blooded murder of Captain Sixkiller, Congress conceded the need to ratify the Major Crimes Act to include legislation that would protect the lives of policemen serving in Indian Territory. According to a letter written by Judge Isaac Parker to the Creek Indian's Chief J. M. Perryman, the murder of Captain Sam Sixkiller was a "brutal, barbarous assassination that has attracted the attention of the whole country." The judge added, "It has been alluded to in debate in the Congress of the Nation." This was the judge's way of preparing Chief Perryman for what was to come.[8]

The Major Crimes Act was enacted by Congress in 1885, after a Sioux Indian named Crow Dog was accused of killing a Sioux Indian named Spotted Tail while on the reservation. Under the traditional rules of the tribe, the chiefs and elders dealt with the matter by making Crow Dog pay restitution to Spotted Tail's family for the murder. But because the incident happened on a reservation overseen by the United States, Crow Dog was arrested for the murder and tried again in a federal court. He was found guilty and sentenced to death.

Crow Dog appealed, claiming his incarceration was illegal because the district court had no jurisdiction to try him. The Supreme Court agreed and ordered Crow Dog released. Distressed by the decision and fearful of the extensive protection the tribal sovereignty provided, Congress drafted the Major Crimes Act.

The initial statute threatened to reduce the internal sovereignty of native tribes by potentially removing their ability to try and to punish serious offenders in Indian Country. The legislation listed seven major crimes that fell under federal jurisdiction and could be tried by the federal government if it chose to intercede: murder, manslaughter, rape, assault with intent to commit murder, arson, burglary, and larceny. Debate over the statute continued for more than a year.[9]

After a ratified edition of the Major Crimes Act was signed into action by President Benjamin Harrison on March 2, 1887, the federal law now specifically addressed the ramification for killing an Indian deputy marshal. Statute number twenty-four read: "Any Indian who commits against the person of any Indian policeman appointed under the laws of the United States, or any Indian United States deputy marshal, while lawfully engaged in the execution of any United States process, or lawfully engaged in any other duty imposed upon such policeman or marshal by the laws of the United States, any of the following crimes, namely, murder, manslaughter, or assault with intent to kill, within the Indian Territory, shall be subject to the laws of the United States relating to such crimes, and shall be tried by the district court of the United States exercising criminal jurisdiction where said offense was committed, and shall be subject to the same penalties as are all other persons charged with the commission of said crimes."[10]

The important and overdue act was seen as a fitting tribute to Captain Sixkiller and the other slain Indian officers who had sacrificed their lives to uphold the law of the Indian Nation.

Judge Isaac Parker was in favor of Congress's decision to sign into effect the appropriation act. He mentioned the government's dedication to the matter in a correspondence with Chiefs Bushyhead and Perryman when he informed them that he had waived the requirements to extradite Cunningham. "This case is one of the most important which has been presented to your court. The murder of Captain Sixkiller was a brutal, barbarous assassination. . . . It has attracted the attention of the whole country. It has been alluded to in debate in the Congress of the Nation."[11]

In July 1887 Alf Cunningham was handcuffed, placed on a horse, and escorted from Fort Smith back to Cherokee officials in Muskogee.

An article in the May 12, 1887, edition of the *Indian Journal* expressed how supporters of the slain US deputy marshal had hoped for such an outcome. "All men are innocent until proven guilty," the article reminded readers. "While every circumstance surrounding the killing of our brave officer Captain Sixkiller connects Alf Cunningham with it, he is now a prisoner in the hands of the law and should receive by fair and impartial trial that justice which is the right of every man. . . . As there have been some insinuations from Fort Smith papers that the Creek wish to move Cunningham to their court first, we desire to state that he will be in more danger at that location and should be sent here initially. Our people want to see the law enforced, and are willing to be patient and abide its delays, feeling sure the present Judge of Muskogee, District Attorney E.H. Lablance, Esq., will see justice is served to all."[12]

On Monday evening, August 1, 1887, Alf Cunningham cast a speculative eye at Willie Sevier, one of the officers standing guard over prisoners to be transported to Muskogee, Oklahoma Territory. Sevier returned the look as he chained the hands of one of the two captives in his charge behind their backs. Horace Schooner, another officer on duty, did the same to Cunningham. Sevier noticed that Cunningham and Schooner were speaking to one another in hushed tones. He walked over to the pair to hear what was being said, and their quiet conversation ended abruptly. Sevier glared at Cunningham, but the felon was unshaken.

Later that evening Schooner approached Sevier in the jail yard with a confession. "I feel kind of sorry for Cunningham," he told the fellow guard. "You ought to let him loose." The request was so preposterous that Sevier responded as though Schooner was teasing. "Sure," Sevier said sarcastically, "and a gold eagle to help him on his way." "He wanted me to give him my key," Schooner offered after a moment's thought, then added, "but I didn't." Sevier studied the man, then snapped back at him, "Don't even act as though you're going to give him that key! No matter how you feel. Your responsibility is to not let Cunningham escape," he warned.[13]

After their discussion Sevier believed Schooner would not allow himself to be taken advantage of by Cunningham, but he was wrong. On August 3, 1887, Cunningham escaped from the Fort Smith jail, and his immediate whereabouts were a mystery. As a result the August 4 hearing that had been scheduled to address his crimes was postponed indefinitely. Cunningham was never recaptured and never stood trial for his part in the brutal murder of Captain Sixkiller.[14]

While authorities were in pursuit of Cunningham in Arkansas, a posse north of the town of Vinita was closing in on Dick Vann. The August 20, 1896, edition of the *Muskogee Phoenix* recalled that Vann and another felon he was traveling with had been apprehended in the summer of 1887. "They had in their possession a number of stolen cattle," the article noted. "During the day Vann escaped from the officers. He was located again . . . and when officers attempted to arrest him he showed that he was going to fight and posse member, Jim Thompson, shot him. Thompson inflicted a wound, which it is thought will prove fatal. Vann has been a terror over about Gibson and Vian (in Oklahoma Territory) for a long time and was regarded as a bad man to handle, having been mixed up in a number of shooting scrapes in the past. The good citizens across the river will breathe easier now that his career has been brought to an end."[15]

The report that the posse had cut Vann's life short was not accurate. In late September 1887 a healthy-looking Vann and his cohort, Chock Cordery, were at Fort Gibson visiting friends and drinking. Vann had decided that he was no longer going to hide from the law or allow himself to be arrested. He knew he would be hanged for murdering Captain Sixkiller and was prepared to shoot it out with the law rather than be executed. Jackson Ellis, deputy marshal in the western district of Arkansas, would fearlessly engage the outlaw in a gunfight. Ellis had a reputation for confronting criminals on the run. He had shot and killed a number of murderers, train robbers, and bootleggers in his career.[16]

At ten o'clock at night on September 20, 1887, Vann and Cordery left their associates' home and walked to the spot outside of town where their horses were waiting for them. As they passed by Deputy Marshal Ellis's home, they pulled their guns and began shooting indiscriminately into the night. "Jackson Ellis, hearing the shots went to a window where he fired his own pistol," the September 28, 1887, edition of the *Cherokee Advocate* reported. "A single shot fired by Ellis struck Dick Vann passing through both of his thighs. Vann walked about one hundred yards where he fell to the ground dying from the loss of blood. Friends took Vann from where he fell to their home seven miles from Fort Gibson where he died."[17]

Fannie Sixkiller and her children were pleased that one of the men responsible for the murder of their husband and father had paid for his actions. Adjusting to life without Captain Sixkiller had been difficult for Fannie. She kept herself busy volunteering at the local school and library, creating shelves for the books she collected for Muskogee County. On May 27, 1889, Fannie passed away, weakened by her grief and debilitated by consumption. News of her demise was reported in several newspapers throughout the Nation, including the *Cherokee Advocate*. "Mrs. Fannie Sixkiller, was the wife of the late Samuel Sixkiller, who met his match two years ago this Christmas. Rev. T. F. Brewer officiated at the funeral in the Methodist Church, and she was laid to rest in the Muskogee City Cemetery." Among the attendees at the funeral were Captain Sixkiller's brother Lieutenant Henry Sixkiller and his family. They had traveled from their home in Eufaula, Oklahoma Territory, to be at the services.[18]

As for Fannie and Captain Sixkiller's children, the oldest of their twin daughters, Rachel, died shortly after her mother, on July 4, 1889.

Photo of Captain Sixkiller's children taken in 1895. From left to right: Cora, Sam Jr., Tookah, Frances Edna. COURTESY OF THE BATY FAMILY

Rachel had struggled for a long time with an unknown illness. Rachel's twin, Eliza, married at the age of fifteen and shortly thereafter gave birth to Fannie and Captain Sixkiller's first grandchild, a girl named Llewellyn Hopewell Morgan. Their youngest daughter, Frances Edna, taught school in Sallisaw, Oklahoma Territory. Eliza, Emma "Tookah," Cora, and James (the captain's son by Mary Malissia Murphey) married and had families of their own. Samuel Jr. followed his father into law enforcement after graduating from Harvard. He built a reputation of his own in the Muskogee area and, like his father before him, was known to all as the "terror of outlaws."[19] "After he had finished his education (in Pennsylvania) he went back to the Indian Territory," a college companion shared with the Milford, Iowa, newspaper the *Milford Mail* on February 7, 1901. "The United States marshal's place in the Indian country was one of great consequence and importance. He must be a man of iron nerve, a quick, deadly shot with the revolver or rifle, and besides all that full of resource and fertility of expediency."[20]

According to the same article, not long after Sam Jr. was made chief deputy marshal for the Indian country, a large quantity of counterfeit money was being filtered into the territory. "The bills were twos, fives, and twenties," the newspaper noted. "So good was the engraving that it was only when the bills were sent to Washington that the counterfeits were discovered." Sam took on the case and within a month located the men who had been passing the phony money to Cherokee, Choctaw, and Creek cattle ranchers. He found that three men who called themselves the Daltons were the main culprits of the crime. They had been known as train robbers prior to this event, but unfortunately the testimony on the counterfeit case was not strong enough to convict them. Two of them were arrested when they were not expecting it.[21]

"They were carrying great quantities of this money on their person, buying cattle, mules, hogs, anything they could," the *Milford Mail* noted. "Sam Sixkiller was warned that he would be killed as his father before him had been. But it made no difference. He went on with his work." Sam Sixkiller Jr. died in 1930 at the age of fifty-three of unknown causes. He was survived by his wife, Martha "Mattie" Bell Sixkiller.[22]

In June 1888 the US Congress amended the Major Crimes Act statute number twenty-four, which protected Native American lawmen, to include other heinous crimes such as rape, arson, burglary, and larceny. If perpetrated against Indian police, the culprit would be punished to the fullest extent of the federal law.[23]

The promise of swift discipline by the US government to protect Native American lawmen like Captain Sam Sixkiller did not readily deter serious offenders from their criminal activities. Even with the legislation in place, the captain's replacement, Deputy Marshal William Fields, was shot and killed three months after taking the job. On April 10, 1887,

Captain Sixkiller's younger son, James, and his family. James is seated in the center wearing a hat, next to his wife, Rosa. COURTESY OF THE BATY FAMILY

Fields was trying to arrest a man named James H. Cunnius for robbing the Missouri Pacific Railroad. After being told he was under arrest, Cunnius drew a shotgun and fired both barrels into Fields. One of the lawmen with the marshal returned fire and shot Cunnius through the leg between the knee and hip. Cunnius surrendered but not before emptying his pistol at the lawmen and missing every time. Authorities confiscated his gun and placed him under arrest.[24]

In time, the Major Crimes Act proved to be effective and was seen by politicians and Indian leaders as a powerful tool to deal with the serious issues of crime and punishment. During the last year in which Captain Sam Sixkiller was a US deputy marshal, twenty-four Indian lawmen were murdered during the discharge of their duties. Their assailants either escaped before their trial and were never tracked down again, were acquitted for their crimes because of lack of evidence, or were shot and killed by other lawbreakers. Morrison Waite, US chief justice, considered the amended law an important step in helping to protect Indian police and a worthy memorial to Captain Sixkiller and his career in law enforcement.[25] "Indian Country is plagued by violent crimes," Chief Justice Waite was quoted as saying in the February 18, 1887, edition of the *Anglo-American Times*. "Captain Sixkiller had been the prevailing person to contain lawlessness throughout the territory. His death will be badly felt. I have great confidence the revised bill will have a positive effect for other great Indian lawmen like him."[26]

Captain Sixkiller was buried at the Methodist Episcopal Church in Muskogee, Oklahoma Territory. Over the years the original structure was torn down and the location of the facility moved. Many of the cemetery's tombstones have crumbled and faded with time—the captain's among them. Nothing marks the lawman's grave now, and his ancestors have no idea of the exact location of his resting place.[27] Nevertheless, the mark that Sam Sixkiller's life and untimely death made on our country's laws will never be erased.

Epilogue

Long after Captain Sixkiller was gone, his absence was still keenly felt by citizens of the Indian Nation and Oklahoma Territory. Newspapers throughout the Indian Nation continued to publish articles about the lawman's effect on the area. On the first anniversary of the captain's burial, the *Indian Journal* shared with readers how much towns like Eufaula regretted not having him around to protect them from the usual ruffians and lawbreakers. "We mourn with the rest of the Territory the loss of Capt. Sam Sixkiller," the December 29, 1887, edition of the paper read. "He was the noblest and best officer this Territory ever had."[1]

On May 15, 1887, the *New York Times* ran an article about Sam Sixkiller and his legacy. The piece referred to the captain as a "Cherokee Dead, Shot" and noted that the Indians who lived and thrived within the borders of the Indian Nation felt safe from harm when Sixkiller was alive.

The bad men of the Territory were more in awe of Sam Sixkiller than of any Indian or white man who stood in boots or moccasins," the commentary began. "He was killed not long ago by a gang who waylaid him. Sixkiller was an extraordinary character in many respects. He was Chief of the Indian Police of the Territory. His regular force numbered 100 men, and he had a reserve of 300 who were always on call.

Sixkiller was a family name. One of his relatives was a cross between John L. Sullivan and Skobeleff as a fighter. In one of the fights between his Nation, the Cherokees and the Creeks, he killed six men and then killed himself. He was called Sixkiller from this little feat, and the name descended from father to son until it reached Sam Sixkiller. He was a worthy descendant of the original Sixkiller. How many men he put under sod is not known, but it is commonly supposed that as an Indian of destruction he could easily discount his fighting ancestor.

Captain Sam was a mixed-blood Cherokee. He was a Knight Templar and paraded with the Knights at their annual encampment at St. Louis last fall. In the light of his achievements and reputation, his appearance was disappointing. In stature he was rather short for his bulk. He stood 5 foot 8 inches in his boots and weighed 220 pounds. He was almost fat, but in spite of his avoirdupois and 45 years was wonderfully agile. His small eyes glittered like black diamonds. Phlegmatic as a fifteenth-century Dutchman he was seldom talkative. He was a man of deeds rather than words. With the rifle or the revolver he was a dead shot. Fatigue he was a stranger to and he was afraid of nothing. When he struck a trail he followed it until he ran the quarry down and more than once when a flying desperado heard that Captain Sam was on his trail he took the backtrack and surrendered.

The fugitive from justice who was caught and gave no further trouble was kindly enough treated, but expeditiously he was carried off the territory road—for Captain Sixkiller had a nice sense of propriety—and left there. The amount of lead he carried depended upon the manner he accepted his fate. It was difficult unless justice inquired after the man who had disappeared, to fasten his fate upon any of Capt. Sam's men; they looked so much alike that to punish the right man it might have been necessary to punish the entire band, and at any rate, they never took the law into their own hands except under great provocation. Sixkiller was in the employ of the Government and under contract with the Indian Agent. His powers were somewhat similar to that of a United States Marshal. His field of action was

*bounded by the limits of the Territory. Capt. Sam was a terror to evil-
doers and his like may never be seen again.[2]*

In recognition of Captain Sixkiller's daring, self-reliance, knowledge, and protection of the Indian Territory, a photograph of the lawman and a list of his accomplishments on the job hang in the lobby of the courthouse in Fort Smith, Arkansas. His picture hangs beside other courageous US deputy marshals like Bass Reeves, Heck Thomas, and Bill Tilghman.

Endnotes

Chapter 1: Comes a Lighthorseman

1. Sam Sixkiller's Confederate Muster Roll, Compiled Military Service File, Ref. #09011001, National Archives & Records Administration.

2. Elbert Little Jr. and Charles Olmsted, *Records of Flowering Plants of Southeastern Oklahoma*, 44.

3. Ned O. Eddins, "Alcohol and the Indian Fur Trade," 1–7; Brad Northrup, "Indians, Whites, and Alcohol," 1–2.

4. Izumi Ishii, *Bad Fruits of the Civilized Tree: Alcohol and the Sovereignty of the Cherokee Nation*, 39–45.

5. Benjamin Franklin, *Autobiography of Benjamin Franklin*, 281.

6. Early Muskogee, Oklahoma History, 1–2.

7. David Dary, *Entrepreneurs of the Old West*, 268–69, Missouri Pacific Railroad, 1–5.

8. Ned O. Eddins, "Alcohol and the Indian Fur Trade," 1–7.

9. Izumi Ishii, *Bad Fruits of the Civilized Tree: Alcohol and the Sovereignty of the Cherokee Nation*, 73.

10. Ibid., 44, 114; Ned O. Eddins, "Alcohol and the Indian Fur Trade," 1–7.

11. Ned O. Eddins, "Alcohol and the Indian Fur Trade," 1–7; Glen Fleischmann, *The Cherokee Removal, 1838: An Entire Indian Nation Is Forced Out of Its Homeland*, 38–39.

12. Ibid., 22–26.

13. Ibid.; John Ehle, *Trail of Tears: The Rise and Fall of the Cherokee Nation*, 16–25; Gloria Jahoda, *The Trail of Tears*, 48.

14. Glen Fleischmann, *The Cherokee Removal, 1838: An Entire Indian Nation Is Forced Out of Its Homeland*, 24–30.

15. Ibid.; Susan Tuddenham, "After the Trail of Tears: The Cherokee in Oklahoma, 1838–1870," 8–14; William Justin, "Harsh Law for Indians," 19–22.

16. Richard Peters, Cherokee Nation vs. State of Georgia, United States Supreme Court Reports, Vol. 1.

17. Glen Fleischmann, *The Cherokee Removal, 1838: An Entire Indian Nation Is Forced Out of Its Homeland*, 35–38.

18. Izumi Ishii, *Bad Fruits of the Civilized Tree: Alcohol and the Sovereignty of the Cherokee Nation*, 75–78.

19. Angie Debo, *Indian Removal: The Emigration of the Five Civilized Tribes of Indians*, 229–32.

20. Ibid., 236.

21. Ibid.; Susan Tuddenham, "After the Trail of Tears: The Cherokee in Oklahoma, 1838–1870," 8–14; William Justin, "Harsh Law for Indians," 19–22.

22. Art T. Burton, "Frontier Indian Police," Part 1, 1–5; *Indian Journal*, March 1, 1883.

23. Ibid.

24. Norman A. Graebner, "Public Land Policy of the Five Civilized Tribes," 107–11.

25. *Indian Journal*, May 24, 1881.

26. Art T. Burton, "Frontier Indian Police," Part 1, 1–5; James Wilson, *The Earth Shall Weep: A History of Native America*, 180–200.

27. Ibid.

28. Art T. Burton, "Frontier Indian Police," Part 1, 1–5.

29. William T. Hagan, *Indian Police and Judges*, 51.

30. Izumi Ishii, *Bad Fruits of the Civilized Tree: Alcohol and the Sovereignty of the Cherokee Nation*, 159–64.

31. Will Chavez, "Cherokee Historic Profiles," cherokeephoenix.org.

32. Cherokee Nation, www.cherokee.org.

33. Joe Scraper Jr., *The Scraper-Sixkiller Book*, 35.

34. United States Senate Document No. 120, 25th Congress.

35. Joe Scraper Jr., *The Scraper-Sixkiller Book*, 35.

36. John and Mary Lou Missall, *The Seminole Wars: America's Longest Indian Conflict*, 63–64.

37. *Huron Reflector*, Huron, Ohio, March 20, 1838.

Chapter 2: Principals of Peace

1. *New York Times*, May 15, 1887.

2. *Statesville Daily Record*, January 18, 1972.

3. *Kingsport Times*, June 14, 1942.

4. *Hutchinson News,* July 13, 1997.

5. *Muskogee Times,* August 5, 1956.

6. Ibid.

7. Ibid.

8. Ibid.

9. Jeanne Williams, *Trail of Tears,* 84; Susan Tuddenham, "After the Trail of Tears: The Cherokee in Oklahoma, 1838–1870," 1–7; Glen Fleischmann, *The Cherokee Removal, 1838: An Entire Indian Nation Is Forced Out of Its Homeland,* 70–72.

10. Constitution of the Cherokee Nation, September 6, 1839.

11. Charles J. Kappler, *Indian Affairs: Law and Treaties,* Vol. II, 561–65.

12. Glen Fleischmann, *The Cherokee Removal, 1838: An Entire Indian Nation Is Forced Out of Its Homeland,* 24–35.

13. Government Report of Communion to Five Civilized Tribes, U.S. Interior Department, 138.

14. Government Court Record, Eastern Band of Cherokee Indians vs. the U.S., March 1, 1886.

15. Ibid.

16. Congressional Recommendation President James K. Polk, April 13, 1846; Susan Tuddenham, "After the Trail of Tears: The Cherokee in Oklahoma, 1838–1870," 6–10.

17. Quote provided by Terry Zinn, history director at Cherokee Nation Cultural Resource Center.

18. Angie Debo and Grant Foreman, *Indian Removal: The Emigration of the Five Civilized Tribes of Indians,* 17–24.

19. Carolyn Thomas Forman, "The Lighthorsemen in the Indian Territory," 17–24.

20. *Cherokee Advocate,* November 11, 1845; *Stillwell Democrat-Journal,* March 16, 1978.

21. Letter to Cherokee agent Colonel J. McKisick from Chief George Lowrey.

22. Emmet Starr, *History of the Cherokee Indians and their Legends and Folklore,* 137–39.

23. Western History Collections, University of Oklahoma, Norman, Oklahoma, M452 Box 5 Folder 2.

24. Joe Scraper Jr., *The Scraper-Sixkiller Book,* 51.

25. *Indian Journal,* December 29, 1886.

26. Western History Collections, University of Oklahoma, Norman, Oklahoma, Bigby PS-149, April 19, 1937.

27. Jeanne Williams, *Trail of Tears*, 178.

28. Western History Collections, University of Oklahoma, Norman, Oklahoma, M452 Box 5 Folder 2.

29. William T. Hagan, *Indian Police and Judges*, 59–60; Glen Fleischmann, *The Cherokee Removal, 1838: An Entire Nation Is Forced Out of Its Homeland*, 10–11.

30. Compiled Military Service File, Ref. #09011001, National Archives & Records Administration.

31. Wayne T. Walker, "Captain Sixkiller–Indian Policeman" *Golden West Magazine*, November 1969.

32. Emma Sixkiller, Western History Collections, University of Oklahoma; Robert Ernst, "Sam Sixkiller: Tragic Life of an Indian Lawman," *Frontier Times Magazine*, October 1984.

33. Ibid.

34. Compiled Military Service File, Ref. #09011001, National Archives & Records Administration; Robert Ernst, "Sam Sixkiller: Tragic Life of an Indian Lawman," *Frontier Times Magazine*, October 1984.

35. Ibid.

36. Ibid.; Jeanne Williams, *Trail of Tears*, 180–82.

37. Joe Scraper Jr., *The Scraper-Sixkiller Book*, 35; William T. Hagan, *Indian Police and Judges*, 59–60.

38. Ibid.

39. Compiled Military Service File, Ref. #09011001, National Archives & Records Administration.

40. Peter Collier, *When Shall They Rest? The Cherokee's Long Struggle with America*, 93–94.

41. Annual Report of the Secretary of the Interior, Serv. 3915, 256.

42. Records of the Indian Division, Office of the Secretary of the Interior, Special File 30-0864.

43. Justin William, "Harsh Law for Indians," *North America Review*, March 1882.

44. *Tahlequah City Directory*, 1896, Indian Territory & Cherokee County, www.filesusgwarchives.net.

45. Wayne T. Walker, "Captain Sixkiller–Indian Policeman" *Golden West Magazine*, November 1969.

46. Ibid.; Joe Scraper Jr., *The Scraper-Sixkiller Book*, 44.

47. Wayne T. Walker, "Captain Sixkiller–Indian Policeman," *Golden West Magazine,* November 1969; Robert Ernst, "Sam Sixkiller: Tragic Life of an Indian Lawman," *Frontier Times Magazine,* October 1984.

48. J. Shannon, Cherokee National Penitentiary, www.cityoftahlequah.

49. Ibid.

50. Wayne T. Walker, "Captain Sixkiller–Indian Policeman," *Golden West Magazine,* November 1969.

51. Ibid.

52. Ibid.

53. William T. Hagan, *Indian Police and Judges,* 62.

Chapter 3: Trouble in Tahlequah

1. Arrest Records for Willis Pettit, United States Court System, Western District of Arkansas Records Department.

2. Tahlequah, www.okstate.edu.

3. Arrest Records for Willis Pettit, United States Court System, Western District of Arkansas Records Department.

4. William L. Katz, *Black Indians: A Hidden Heritage,* 143–47.

5. Robert Ernst, "Sam Sixkiller: Tragic Life of an Indian Lawman," *Frontier Times Magazine,* October 1984.

6. *Cherokee Advocate,* November 25, 1876; *Muskogee Phoenix,* October 27, 1894; *Indian Journal,* February 12, 1880.

7. Ibid.; Wayne T. Walker, "Captain Sixkiller–Indian Policeman," *Golden West Magazine,* November 1969.

8. *Cherokee Advocate,* April 11, 1877.

9. Ibid.

10. Will Chavez, "Cherokee Historic Profiles," www.cherokeephoenix.org; Art T. Burton, "Black, Red and Deadly, Part II," Art Burton's Wild West, www.artburton .com; Luke Sixkiller Interview #373, University of Oklahoma, Western History Collection; Robert B. Thomas, *Farmer's Almanac,* Fall 1878.

11. Wayne T. Walker, "Captain Sixkiller–Indian Policeman," *Golden West Magazine,* November 1969; Joseph T. Hallinan, *Going Up the River: Travels in a Prison Nation,* 87–94.

12. Robert Ernst, "Sam Sixkiller: Tragic Life of an Indian Lawman," *Frontier Times Magazine,* October 1984.

13. Wayne T. Walker, "Captain Sixkiller–Indian Policeman" *Golden West Magazine,* November 1969.

14. William T. Hagan, *Indian Police and Judges,* 60.

15. *Cherokee Advocate,* November 30, 1878.

16. *Indian Journal,* December 5, 1878.

17. Wayne T. Walker, "Captain Sixkiller-Indian Policeman," *Golden West Magazine,* November 1969.

18. *Indian Journal,* December 5, 1878.

19. J. Shannon, Cherokee National Penitentiary, www.cityoftahlequah.com.

20. *Cherokee Advocate*, November 30, 1878.

21. Ibid.

22. J. Shannon, Cherokee National Penitentiary, www.cityoftahlequah.com.

23. Arrest Records for Solomon Coon, United States Court Systems, Western District of Arkansas Records Department.

24. *Cherokee Advocate,* June 11, 1879.

25. Ibid.

26. J. Shannon, Cherokee National Penitentiary, www.cityoftahlequah.com.

27. *Cherokee Advocate,* July 23, 1879.

28. *Cherokee Advocate,* June 18, 1879; J. Shannon, Cherokee National Penitentiary, www.cityoftahlequah.com.

29. Charles Baty (great-great-grandson of Sam Sixkiller), telephone interview, July 12, 2010; *Indian Journal,* May 25, 1889.

30. *Cherokee Advocate,* June 30, 1879.

31. Cherokee Nation, www.cherokee.org, CHN II Vol. 270, 166.

32. Ibid.

33. *Cherokee Advocate,* August 20, 1879.

34. Cherokee Nation, www.cherokee.org, CHN 12 Vol. 275A, 116; Glen Fleischmann, *The Cherokee Removal, 1838: An Entire Indian Nation Is Forced Out of Its Homeland,* 25–32.

35. Robert Ernst, "Sam Sixkiller: Tragic Life of an Indian Lawman," *Frontier Times Magazine,* October 1984.

36. Wayne T. Walker, "Captain Sixkiller–Indian Policeman" *Golden West Magazine,* November 1969.

Chapter 4: Mayhem in Muskogee

1. Robert B. Thomas, *Farmer's Almanac,* Spring 1880.

2. Early Muskogee, Oklahoma History, 2–7.

3. Izumi Ishii, *Bad Fruits of the Civilized Tree: Alcohol and the Sovereignty of the Cherokee Nation,* 115.

4. Wayne T. Walker, "Captain Sixkiller–Indian Policeman" *Golden West Magazine,* November 1969.

5. Jan MacKell, *Brothels, Bordellos, and Bad Girls: Prostitution in Colorado 1860–1930,* 20.

6. Ibid.; Wayne T. Walker, "Captain Sixkiller–Indian Policeman" *Golden West Magazine,* November 1969.

7. Robert Ernst, "Sam Sixkiller: Tragic Life of an Indian Lawman," *Frontier Times Magazine,* October 1984.

8. *Indian Journal,* February 12, 1880; *Indian Journal,* July 12, 1880.

9. Robert Ernst, "Sam Sixkiller: Tragic Life of an Indian Lawman," *Frontier Times Magazine,* October 1984.

10. Wayne T. Walker, "Captain Sixkiller–Indian Policeman" *Golden West Magazine,* November 1969.

11. Ibid.

12. Letter from Indian Agent Robert L. Owens to Secretary of State James G. Blaine, December 29, 1886.

13. *Indian Journal,* February 12, 1880.

14. *Indian Chieftain,* Vinita, April 24, 1884; Early Muskogee, Oklahoma History, 2–7; Wayne T. Walker, "Captain Sixkiller–Indian Policeman" *Golden West Magazine,* November 1969.

15. Miriam Allen de Ford, *They Were San Franciscans,* 266.

16. Jay Gould Biography, www.biography.com; Jay Gould, www.wikipedia.com.

17. *Indian Journal,* June 5, 1884.

18. Early Muskogee, Oklahoma History, 2–7; Art T. Burton, "Frontier Indian Police," Part 1, 1–5.

19. Arrest Records for Willis Pettit, United States Court System, Western District of Arkansas Records Department.

20. Ibid.

21. Arrest Records for Henry Blake, United States Court System, Western District of Arkansas Records Department.

22. *Galveston Daily News,* September 9, 1894.

23. Ibid.

24. Ibid.

25. Ibid.

26. William T. Hagan, *Indian Police and Judges,* 6–15.

27. James Crutchfield and Bill and Walker O'Neal, *Legends of the Wild West,* 98–100.

28. Arrest Records for Nathan Harris, United States Court System, Western District of Arkansas Records Department.

29. *Indian Journal,* March 11, 1881.

30. *Indian Journal,* March 18, 1881.

31. Arrest Records for W. R. Fox, United States Court System, Western District of Arkansas Records Department.

32. *Indian Journal,* October 11, 1881.

33. Arrest Records for Frank Woods, United States Court System, Western District of Arkansas Records Department.

34. Ibid.

35. William T. Hagan, *Indian Police and Judges,* 51–60; Jay Robert Nash, *Encyclopedia of Western Lawmen & Outlaws,* 252–53; Candy Moulton, *Everyday Life in the Wild West: From 1840–1900,* 269.

36. Arrest Records for Charles Ashcroft, United States Court System, Western District of Arkansas Records Department.

37. Arrest Records for Frank Jones, United States Court System, Western District of Arkansas Records Department.

38. Ibid.

39. Izumi Ishii, *Bad Fruits of the Civilized Tree: Alcohol and the Sovereignty of the Cherokee Nation,* 115; Missouri Pacific Railroad, www.katyrailroad.org.

40. *New York Times,* January 20, 1888.

41. Arrest Records for Barney Sweeny, United States Court System, Western District of Arkansas Records Department.

42. Telegram from Captain Sam Sixkiller to Fort Smith marshals, September 15, 1882.

43. Thomas Furlong, *Fifty Years a Detective,* 258.

44. Ibid.; *Grand Rapid Tribune,* January 12, 1888; *New York Times,* January 20, 1888.

45. Thomas Furlong, *Fifty Years a Detective,* 264.

46. *Iola Register,* February 5, 1883.

47. *Indian Journal,* December 7, 1882.

Chapter 5: Defending the Nation

1. Wayne T. Walker, "Captain Sixkiller–Indian Policeman" *Golden West Magazine,* November 1969.

2. Ibid.; Robert B. Thomas, *Farmer's Almanac,* 1883; Art T. Burton, *The Cherokee Frontier Police of the Indian Territory,* 1–8.

3. Wayne T. Walker, "Captain Sixkiller–Indian Policeman" *Golden West Magazine,* November 1969; Robert Ernst, "Sam Sixkiller: Tragic Life of an Indian Lawman," *Frontier Times Magazine,* October 1984.

4. Izumi Ishii, *Bad Fruits of the Civilized Tree: Alcohol and the Sovereignty of the Cherokee Nation,* 115–29.

5. Letter from Chief Lewis Downing to Indian agent J. B. Jones, July 19, 1872; Emory McGuire, Oklahoma Historical Society, Vol. 7, 53–54.

6. Ibid.

7. Arrest Records for Solomon Coon, United States Court System, Western District of Arkansas Records Department.

8. Ibid.

9. *Indian Journal,* March 29, 1883.

10. *Indian Journal,* September 10, 1885; *Cherokee Advocate,* September 11, 1885.

11. Ibid.

12. Ibid.

13. Ibid.

14. Ibid.

15. Ibid.

16. *Indian Journal,* March 30, 1883.

17. *Indian Journal,* March 30, 1884.

18. Ibid.

19. *Indian Journal,* March 27, 1883.

20. *Indian Journal,* March 20, 1884.

21. Arrest Records for Isaac Deer, United States Court System, Western District of Arkansas Records Department.

22. Ibid.; Izumi Ishii, *Bad Fruits of the Civilized Tree: Alcohol and the Sovereignty of the Cherokee Nation,* 115–29.

23. Ibid., 42–44.

24. Arrest Records for Isaac Deer, United States Court System, Western District of Arkansas Records Department.

25. Ibid.; *Petersburg Daily Index-Appeal,* February 2, 1887; *Indian Journal,* July 7, 1884.

26. *Indian Journal,* November 20, 1884.

27. Ibid.

28. Railroad History, Oklahoma Hombres, www.oklahoma.org; Charles Baty (great-great-grandson of Sam Sixkiller), telephone interview, July 12, 2010.

29. *Indian Journal,* April 12, 1883.

30. Ibid.

31. *Indian Journal,* January 29, 1885.

32. Harold Preece, *The Dalton Gang,* 74–85; The Dalton Gang, www.theoutlaws.com.

33. *Indian Journal,* February 2, 1885.

34. *Indian Journal,* April 8, 1885.

35. *Indian Journal,* June 5, 1885.

36. *Indian Journal,* June 11, 1885.

37. *Tulsa Daily Democrat,* September 28, 1885.

38. *Indian Journal,* April 23, 1885.

39. Ibid.; D. W. Benson Interview #7616, University of Oklahoma, Western History Collection, Norman, Oklahoma; Badman Dick Glass, www.rootsweb.ancestory.com; Wayne T. Walker, "Captain Sixkiller–Indian Policeman" *Golden West Magazine,* November 1969.

Chapter 6: Badman Dick Glass

1. H. W. Hicks Interview #7605, University of Oklahoma, Western History Collection, Norman, Oklahoma; *Indian Journal,* February 5, 1885.

2. *Indian Journal,* April 2, 1885.

3. D. F. Benson Interview #7616, University of Oklahoma, Western History Collection, Norman, Oklahoma; Dan Anderson, Laurence Yadon, and Robert B. Smith, *100 Oklahoma Outlaws, Gangsters, and Lawmen,* 256–57.

4. H. W. Hicks Interview #7605, University of Oklahoma, Western History Collection, Norman, Oklahoma.

5. William T. Hagan, *Indian Police and Judges,* 62–63; *Indian Journal,* April 2, 1885.

6. Ibid.

7. Dan Anderson, Laurence Yadon, and Robert B. Smith, *100 Oklahoma Outlaws, Gangsters, and Lawmen,* 256–57.

8. *Indian Journal,* April 2, 1885.

9. H. W. Hicks Interview #7605, University of Oklahoma, Western History Collection, Norman, Oklahoma; Freestone, Texas, Criminal Records, Sheriff's Report 1965–2001.

10. Art T. Burton, "Frontier Indian Police," Part 2; Badman Dick Glass, www.rootsweb.ancestry.com.

11. *Indian Journal,* April 2, 1885.

12. Lu Ferguson Interview #6990, University of Oklahoma, Western History Collection, Norman, Oklahoma; Art T. Burton, "Black, Red and Deadly, Part II," Art Burton's Wild West, http://artburton.com.

13. H. W. Hicks Interview #7605, University of Oklahoma, Western History Collection, Norman, Oklahoma; Dick Glass, www.digitallibrary.okstate.edu.

14. Art T. Burton, *Black, Buckskin, and Blue: African American Scouts and Soldiers on the Western Frontier,* 167–69.

15. Dan Anderson, Laurence Yadon, and Robert B. Smith, *100 Oklahoma Outlaws, Gangsters, and Lawmen,* 256–57; H. W. Hicks Interview #7605, University of Oklahoma, Western History Collection, Norman, Oklahoma.

16. Ibid.; Lu Ferguson Interview #6990, University of Oklahoma, Western History Collection, Norman, Oklahoma; Wayne T. Walker, "Captain Sixkiller–Indian Policeman" *Golden West Magazine,* November 1969.

17. *Indian Journal,* June 11, 1885; H. W. Hicks Interview #7605, University of Oklahoma, Western History Collection, Norman, Oklahoma.

18. *Indian Journal,* June 11, 1885; Robert Ernst, "Sam Sixkiller: Tragic Life of an Indian Lawman," *Frontier Times Magazine,* October 1984.

19. Ibid.; Dan Anderson, Laurence Yadon, and Robert B. Smith, *100 Oklahoma Outlaws, Gangsters, and Lawmen,* 256–57.

20. Wayne T. Walker, "Captain Sixkiller–Indian Policeman" *Golden West Magazine,* November 1969.

21. Arrest Records for Jeff Bollen, United States Court System, Western District of Arkansas Records Department.

22. Ibid.

23. Ibid.

24. Wayne T. Walker, "Captain Sixkiller–Indian Policeman" *Golden West Magazine,* November 1969; Robert Ernst, "Sam Sixkiller: Tragic Life of an Indian Lawman," *Frontier Times Magazine,* October 1984.

25. *Indian Journal,* April, 12, 1883.

26. *Indian Journal,* May 29, 1884; Webber Falls, Oklahoma, www.wikipedia.org.

27. Arrest Records for Richard Vann, United States Court System, Western District of Arkansas Records Department.

28. Ibid.

29. Arrest Records for Milo Hoyt, United States Court System, Western District of Arkansas Records Department.

30. *Fort Wayne Sentinel,* July 3, 1884; *Cherokee Advocate,* July 11, 1884.

31. *Indian Journal,* April 16, 1885; *Indian Journal,* September 30, 1886.

32. *Indian Journal,* October 6, 1877; *Indian Journal,* August 19, 1880; *Indian Journal,* May 26, 1887.

33. *Indian Journal,* April 16, 1885; *Indian Journal,* September 30, 1886.

Chapter 7: Keeping the Peace

1. *Indian Journal,* January 28, 1886.

2. Ibid.

3. The Officer Down Memorial Page, www.odmp.org.

4. Wortham, Texas, www.wikipedia.org.

5. Ibid.; Arrest Records for Alf Cunningham aka Ed Brown, United States Court System, Western District of Arkansas Records Department.

6. *Galveston Daily News,* December 4, 1877.

7. *Galveston Daily News,* December 17, 1877.

8. Ibid.; Freestone Past/Present, www.usgwarchives.net.

9. *Indian Journal,* December 28, 1886.

10. Ibid.

11. Freestone Past/Present, www.usgwarchives.net; *Indian Journal,* August 26, 1880.

12. Ibid.

13. *Milford Mail,* February 7, 1901.

14. Ibid.; Charles Baty (great-great-grandson of Sam Sixkiller), telephone interview, July 12, 2010.

15. *Milford Mail,* February 7, 1901.

16. *Tyrone Daily Herald,* November 17, 1901.

17. *Salina Journal,* June 8, 1952; *Titusville Herald,* March 26, 1971.

18. Ibid.

19. *Indian Journal,* August 16, 1883.

20. Ibid.; Izumi Ishii, *Bad Fruits of the Civilized Tree: Alcohol and the Sovereignty of the Cherokee Nation,* 115–28.

21. *Muskogee Phoenix,* February 26, 1885.

22. Ibid.; Arrest Records for (First Name Unknown) Wright, United States Court System, Western District of Arkansas Records Department.

23. Ibid.

24. Ibid.

25. William T. Hagan, *Indian Police and Judges,* 66–68.

26. *Indian Journal,* September 9, 1885.

27. Ibid.

28. Ibid.

Chapter 8: Difficulties with Dick Vann

1. *Indian Journal,* May 1, 1916.

2. Ibid.

3. Ibid.; Wayne T. Walker, "Captain Sixkiller–Indian Policeman," *Golden West Magazine,* November 1969.

4. *Indian Journal,* June 17, 1886.

5. Ibid.

6. *Indian Chieftain,* September 23, 1886; Robert Ernst, "Sam Sixkiller: Tragic Life of an Indian Lawman," *Frontier Times Magazine,* October 1984.

7. *Indian Journal,* June 18, 1882; *Indian Journal,* October 12, 1882; *Evening Observer,* July 17, 1884; *Richmond Gazette,* July 10, 1884.

8. Arrest Records for Milo Hoyt, United States Court System, Western District of Arkansas Records Department.

9. *Indian Chieftain,* September 23, 1886; Wayne T. Walker, "Captain Sixkiller–Indian Policeman," *Golden West Magazine,* November 1969; Arrest Records for Richard Vann, United States Court System, Western District of Arkansas Records Department.

10. Ibid.

11. *Indian Chieftain,* September 23, 1886.

12. Arrest Records for Richard Vann, United States Court System, Western District of Arkansas Records Department.

13. *Indian Journal,* August 21, 1884.

14. *Muskogee Phoenix,* February 24, 1898.

15. Ibid.

16. Arrest Records for Richard Vann, United States Court System, Western District of Arkansas Records Department; Webber Falls, Oklahoma, www.wikipedia.org.

17. *Indian Journal,* December 16, 1886.

18. *Indian Journal,* December 22, 1886; *Golden West Magazine,* November 1969; Arrest Records for Richard Vann, United States Court System, Western District of Arkansas Records Department.

19. Ibid.

Chapter 9: A Terrible Tragedy

1. *Indian Journal,* December 29, 1886.

2. Ibid.; William T. Hagan, *Indian Police and Judges,* 64–68.

3. *Indian Journal,* December 29, 1886; *Golden West Magazine,* November 1969.

4. Ibid.; *Indian Chieftain,* December 30, 1886.

5. *Indian Journal,* December 29, 1883; *Cherokee Advocate,* January 5, 1887.

6. Ibid.

7. *Golden West Magazine,* November 1969; William T. Hagan, *Indian Police and Judges,* 64–68; *Indian Journal,* December 15, 1886.

8. Ibid.; *Cherokee Advocate,* January 5, 1887; Robert Ernst, "Sam Sixkiller: Tragic Life of an Indian Lawman," *Frontier Times Magazine,* October 1984.

9. *Indian Journal,* December 29, 1886; *Cherokee Advocate,* January 5, 1887; *Golden West Magazine,* November 1969; William T. Hagan, *Indian Police and Judges,* 64–68.

10. *Golden West Magazine,* November 1969; *Indian Journal,* December 29, 1886.

11. Ibid.

12. Arrest Records for Richard Vann, United States Court System, Western District of Arkansas Records Department; Arrest Records for Alf Cunningham, United States Court System, Western District of Arkansas Records Department.

13. Arrest Records for Richard Vann, United States Court System, Western District of Arkansas Records Department; *Indian Journal,* December 29, 1886.

14. Ibid.

15. Thomas Furlong, *Fifty Years a Detective,* 264–68; *Golden West Magazine,* November 1969; Robert Ernst, "Sam Sixkiller: Tragic Life of an Indian Lawman," *Frontier Times Magazine,* October 1984.

16. *Cherokee Advocate,* January 5, 1887; William T. Hagan, *Indian Police and Judges,* 66–70.

17. Ibid., 66–67; *Indian Journal,* December 29, 1886; *Daily Northwestern,* January 11, 1901.

18. *Cherokee Advocate,* January 5, 1887; "Sam Sixkiller: Tragic Life of an Indian Lawman," *Frontier Times Magazine,* October 1984; *Golden West Magazine,* November 1969; *Indian Journal,* December 29, 1886.

19. *Atchinson Daily Globe,* January 5, 1887.

20. Ibid.; Arrest Records for Richard Vann, United States Court System, Western District of Arkansas Records Department; *Indian Journal,* December 29, 1886.

21. Arrest Records for Alf Cunningham, United States Court System, Western District of Arkansas Records Department; *Indian Journal,* December 29, 1886; "Sam Sixkiller: Tragic Life of an Indian Lawman," *Frontier Times Magazine,* October 1984; *Golden West Magazine,* November 1969; *Indian Journal,* December 29, 1886; William T. Hagan, *Indian Police and Judges,* 66–70.

22. Art T. Burton, *Black, Red and Deadly: Black and Indian Gunfighters of the Indian Territory,* 118–125; United States Marshals Service–Roll Call of Honor, www.okolja.net.

23. *Muskogee Phoenix,* February 24, 1887.

24. *Muskogee Phoenix,* July 11, 1888; *Fort Gibson Post,* November 10, 1898.

25. Margaret Sixkiller Bagby Interview #T-559-3, University of Oklahoma, Western History Collection, Norman, Oklahoma; Charles Baty (great-great-grandson of Sam Sixkiller), telephone interview, July 12, 2010.

Chapter 10: Chasing Assassins

1. *Indian Journal,* January 12, 1887.
2. Ibid.; *Indian Journal,* March 2, 1887; *Indian Journal,* March 16, 1887.
3. Ibid.
4. *Indian Journal,* January 28, 1887; Arrest Records for Alf Cunningham aka Ed Brown, United States Court System, Western District of Arkansas Records; *Indian Chieftain,* April 28, 1887; Wayne T. Walker, "Captain Sixkiller–Indian Policeman," *Golden West Magazine,* November 1969; "Trail of Tears," www.wikipedia.org.
5. *Indian Journal,* May 19, 1887.
6. Arrest Records for Richard Vann, United States Court System, Western District of Arkansas Records.
7. *Indian Journal,* June 23, 1887.
8. William T. Hagan, *Indian Police and Judges,* 62–67; Letter to Chief Perryman from Judge Isaac Parker, May 3, 1887.
9. United States Senate Document No. 120, 25th Congress; Linda Lacey, "The White Man's Law and the American Indian Family in Assimilation Era," *Arkansas Law Review 40,* 327
10. Ibid.
11. William T. Hagan, *Indian Police and Judges,* 62–67; Letter to Chief Perryman from Judge Isaac Parker, May 3, 1887.
12. *Indian Journal,* May 12, 1887.
13. Arrest Records for Alf Cunningham aka Ed Brown, United States Court System, Western District of Arkansas Records; Wayne T. Walker, "Captain Sixkiller–Indian Policeman" *Golden West Magazine,* November 1969.
14. Ibid.
15. *Muskogee Phoenix,* August 20, 1896.
16. *Cherokee Advocate,* September 28, 1887.
17. Ibid.
18. *Muskogee Phoenix,* May 27, 1889; *Indian Journal,* May 30, 1889.
19. *Fort Gibson Post,* February 15, 1900; *Argus,* November 11, 1898.
20. *Milford Mail,* February 7, 1901.
21. Ibid.
22. Ibid.

23. United States Senate Document No. 120, 25th Congress; William T. Hagan, *Indian Police and Judges*, 66–67.

24. OK-Lawman-Outlaw-L Archives, www.listsearch.rootsweb.com.

25. William T. Hagan, *Indian Police and Judges*, 62–67.

26. *Anglo-American Times*, February 18, 1887.

27. Charles Baty (great-great-grandson of Sam Sixkiller), telephone interview, July 12, 2010.

Epilogue

1. *Indian Journal*, December 29, 1887.

2. *New York Times*, May 15, 1887.

Bibliography

Books

Allen de Ford, Miriam. *They Were San Franciscans.* Caldwell, ID: Caxton Printers, 1947.

Anderson, Dan, and Laurence Yadon. *Profiles of Oklahoma Outlaws, Gangsters, and Lawmen.* Gretna, LA: Pelican Publishing, 2007.

Baird, David W. *Historic Context for the Native American Theme Management Region #3, 1830–1941.*

Bettmann, Otto L. *The Good Old Days-They Were Terrible.* New York: Random House, 1974.

Burton, Art T. *Black, Buckskin, and Blue: African American Scouts and Soldiers on the Western Frontier.* Austin, TX: Eakin Press, 1999.

Burton, Art T. *Black, Red and Deadly: Black and Indian Gunfighters of the Indian Territory.* Austin, TX: Eakin Press, 1991.

Campbell, O. B., and I. T. Vinita. *The Story of a Frontier Town of the Cherokee Nation 1871–1907.* Oklahoma City: Colorgraphics, 1969.

Collier, Peter. *When Shall They Rest? The Cherokee's Long Struggle with America.* New York: Dell Publishing, 1975.

Conley, Robert J. *A Cherokee Encyclopedia.* Albuquerque: University of New Mexico Press, 2007.

Crutchfield, James, and O'Neal, Bill and Walker. *Legends of the Wild West.* Lincolnwood, Illinois: Publication International, Inc. 1995

Dary, David. *Entrepreneurs of the Old West.* New York: Alfred A. Knopf, 1986.

Debo, Angie, and Grant Foreman. *Indian Removal: The Emigration of the Five Civilized Tribes of Indians.* Norman: University of Oklahoma, 1974.

Ehle, John. *Trail of Tears: The Rise and Fall of the Cherokee Nation.* New York: Doubleday, 1989.

Fleischmann, Glen. *The Cherokee Removal, 1838: An Entire Indian Nation Is Forced Out of Its Homeland.* New York: Franklin Watts, Inc., 1971.

Franklin, Benjamin. *Autobiography of Ben Franklin.* New York: Tribecca Books, 1994.

Furlong, Thomas. *Fifty Years a Detective.* Charleston, SC: Nabu Press, 2010.

Hagan, William T. *Indian Police and Judges.* Lincoln: University of Nebraska Press, 1966.

Hallinan, Joseph T. *Going Up the River: Travels in a Prison Nation.* New York, New York: Random House Trade Publications, 2003.

Hendricks, George. *The Badman of the West.* San Antonio, TX: The Naylor Company, 1942.

Ishii, Izumi. *Bad Fruits of the Civilized Tree: Alcohol and the Sovereignty of the Cherokee Nation.* Lincoln: University of Nebraska Press, 2008.

Jahoda, Gloria. *The Trail of Tears.* New York: Holt, Rinehart and Winston, 1975.

Johnson, Dorothy M. *Famous Lawmen of the Old West.* New York: Dodd, Mead & Company, 1963.

Katz, William L. *Black Indians: A Hidden Heritage.* New York: Aladdin Paperbacks, 1997.

———. *Black West: A Documentary and Pictorial History of the African American Role in the Westward Expansion of the United States.* New York: Harlem Moon/Broadway Books, 2005.

Little, Elbert Jr., and Charles Olmsted. *Records of Flowering Plants of Southeastern Oklahoma.* Tulsa: Oklahoma Forest Service, 1930.

MacKell, Jan. *Brothels, Bordellos, and Bad Girls: Prostitution in Colorado, 1860–1930.* Albuquerque: University of New Mexico, 2004.

Missall, John and Mary Lou. *The Seminole Wars: America's Longest Indian Conflict.* Gainesville: University of Florida Press, 2004.

Moulton, Candy. *Everyday Life in the Wild West: From 1840–1900.* Cincinnati: Writer's Digest Books, 1999.

Nash, Jay Robert. *Encyclopedia of Western Lawmen & Outlaws.* New York: Paragon House, 1989.

Preece, Harold. *The Dalton Gang.* New York: Signet Books, 1964.

Russell, Don. *The Book of the American West: Indians and Soldiers of the American West.* New York: Simon & Schuster, 1969.

Scraper, Joe Jr. *The Scraper-Sixkiller Book.* Topeka, KS: Scraper Publishing, 2009.

Starr, Emmet. *History of the Cherokee Indians and Their Legends and Folklore.* Baltimore: Genealogical Publishing Company, 2008.

Williams, Jeanne: *Trail of Tears.* New York: Putnam's Sons, 1972.

Wilson, James. *The Earth Shall Weep: A History of Native America.* New York: Grove Press, 1998.

Yancey, Diane. *Desperadoes and Dynamite: Train Robbery in the United States.* New York: Franklin Watts, 1991.

NEWSPAPERS

Anglo-American Times, London, England, February 18, 1887.

Argus, Ontario, Oregon, November 16, 1898.

Atchison Daily Globe, Atchison, Kansas, January 5, 1887.

Cherokee Advocate, Tahlequah, Oklahoma, November 18, 1845.

Cherokee Advocate, Tahlequah, Oklahoma, November 25, 1876.

Cherokee Advocate, Tahlequah, Oklahoma, April 11, 1877.

Cherokee Advocate, Tahlequah, Oklahoma, November 30, 1878.

Cherokee Advocate, Tahlequah, Oklahoma, June 11, 1879.

Cherokee Advocate, Tahlequah, Oklahoma, June 18, 1879.

Cherokee Advocate, Tahlequah, Oklahoma, June 23, 1879.

Cherokee Advocate, Tahlequah, Oklahoma, June 30, 1879.

Cherokee Advocate, Tahlequah, Oklahoma, August 20, 1879.

Cherokee Advocate, Tahlequah, Oklahoma, July 11, 1884.

Cherokee Advocate, Tahlequah, Oklahoma, September 28, 1887.

Daily Northwestern, Evanston, Illinois, January 11, 1901.

Evening Observer, Dunkirk, New York, July 17, 1884.

Female Seminary, Cherokee Nation, Tahlequah, Oklahoma,
    August 3, 1855.

Fort Gibson Post, Fort Gibson, Oklahoma, November 10, 1898.

Fort Wayne Sentinel, Fort Wayne, Indiana, July 3, 1884.

Galesburg Register-Mail, Galesburg, Illinois, December 5, 1972.

Galveston Daily News, Galveston, Texas, December 25, 1866.

Galveston Daily News, Galveston, Texas, December 4, 1877.

Galveston Daily News, Galveston, Texas, December 17, 1877.

Galveston Daily News, Galveston, Texas, September 9, 1894.

Grand Rapids Tribune, Grand Rapids, Wisconsin, April 12, 1881.

Huron Reflector, Huron, Ohio, March 20, 1838.

Hutchinson News, Hutchinson, Kansas, July 13, 1997.

Indian Chieftain, Vinita, Indian Territory, Oklahoma, April 24, 1884.

Indian Chieftain, Vinita, Indian Territory, Oklahoma, September 23,
    1886.

Indian Chieftain, Vinita, Indian Territory, Oklahoma, September 30,
    1886.

Indian Journal, Eufaula, Creek Nation, October 6, 1877.

Indian Journal, Eufaula, Creek Nation, February 13, 1878.

Indian Journal, Eufaula, Creek Nation, May 19, 1887.

Indian Journal, Muskogee, Oklahoma, December 5, 1878.

Indian Journal, Muskogee, Oklahoma, November 13, 1879.

Indian Journal, Muskogee, Oklahoma, February 12, 1880.

Indian Journal, Muskogee, Oklahoma, July 12, 1880.

Indian Journal, Muskogee, Oklahoma, August 19, 1880.

Indian Journal, Muskogee, Oklahoma, August 26, 1880.

Indian Journal, Muskogee, Oklahoma, March 8, 1881.

Indian Journal, Muskogee, Oklahoma, March 18, 1881.

Indian Journal, Muskogee, Oklahoma, May 25, 1881.

Indian Journal, Muskogee, Oklahoma, August 11, 1881.

Indian Journal, Muskogee, Oklahoma, October 11, 1881.

Indian Journal, Muskogee, Oklahoma, June 18, 1882.

Indian Journal, Muskogee, Oklahoma October 12, 1882.

Indian Journal, Muskogee, Oklahoma December 7, 1882.

Indian Journal, Muskogee, Oklahoma March 1, 1883.

Indian Journal, Muskogee, Oklahoma March 20, 1883.

Indian Journal, Muskogee, Oklahoma March 27, 1883.

Indian Journal, Muskogee, Oklahoma March 29, 1883.

Indian Journal, Muskogee, Oklahoma March 30, 1883.

Indian Journal, Muskogee, Oklahoma April 12, 1883.

Indian Journal, Muskogee, Oklahoma May 24, 1883.

Indian Journal, Muskogee, Oklahoma August 16, 1883.

Indian Journal, Muskogee, Oklahoma March 20, 1884.

Indian Journal, Muskogee, Oklahoma March 30, 1884.

Indian Journal, Muskogee, Oklahoma May 1, 1884.

Indian Journal, Muskogee, Oklahoma May 29, 1884.

Indian Journal, Muskogee, Oklahoma June 5, 1884.

Indian Journal, Muskogee, Oklahoma August 21, 1884.

Indian Journal, Muskogee, Oklahoma November 20, 1884.

Indian Journal, Muskogee, Oklahoma January 22, 1885.

Indian Journal, Muskogee, Oklahoma January 29, 1885.

Indian Journal, Muskogee, Oklahoma February 2, 1885.

Indian Journal, Muskogee, Oklahoma February 5, 1885.

Indian Journal, Muskogee, Oklahoma April 2, 1885.

Indian Journal, Muskogee, Oklahoma April 9, 1885.

Indian Journal, Muskogee, Oklahoma April 16, 1885.

Indian Journal, Muskogee, Oklahoma April 23, 1885.

Indian Journal, Muskogee, Oklahoma June 5, 1885.

Indian Journal, Muskogee, Oklahoma June 11, 1885.

Indian Journal, Muskogee, Oklahoma September 10, 1885.

Indian Journal, Muskogee, Oklahoma December 17, 1885.

Indian Journal, Muskogee, Oklahoma January 28, 1886.

Indian Journal, Muskogee, Oklahoma June 17, 1886.

Indian Journal, Muskogee, Oklahoma September 30, 1886.

Indian Journal, Muskogee, Oklahoma October 15, 1886.

Indian Journal, Muskogee, Oklahoma November 15, 1886.

Indian Journal, Muskogee, Oklahoma November 17, 1886.

Indian Journal, Muskogee, Oklahoma December 15, 1886.

Indian Journal, Muskogee, Oklahoma December 16, 1886.

Indian Journal, Muskogee, Oklahoma December 29, 1886.

Indian Journal, Muskogee, Oklahoma January 2, 1887.

Indian Journal, Muskogee, Oklahoma January 12, 1887.

Indian Journal, Muskogee, Oklahoma January 28, 1887.

Indian Journal, Muskogee, Oklahoma March 2, 1887.

Indian Journal, Muskogee, Oklahoma March 16, 1887.

Indian Journal, Muskogee, Oklahoma May 12, 1887.

Indian Journal, Muskogee, Oklahoma May 24, 1887.

Indian Journal, Muskogee, Oklahoma May 25, 1887.

Indian Journal, Muskogee, Oklahoma May 26, 1887.

Indian Journal, Muskogee, Oklahoma June 23, 1887.

Indian Journal, Muskogee, Oklahoma July 7, 1887.

Indian Journal, Muskogee, Oklahoma August 2, 1887.

Indian Journal, Muskogee, Oklahoma September 23, 1887.

Indian Journal, Muskogee, Oklahoma December 29, 1887

Indian Journal, Muskogee, Oklahoma March 23, 1888.

Indian Journal, Muskogee, Oklahoma May 25, 1889.

Indian Journal, Muskogee, Oklahoma May 30, 1889.

Indian Journal, Muskogee, Oklahoma May 1, 1916.

Iola Register, Iola, Kansas September 22, 1882.

Kingsport Times, Kingsport, Tennessee, June 14, 1942.

Logansport Journal, Logansport, Indiana, July 7, 1884.

Milford Mail, Milford, Iowa, February 7, 1901.

Muskogee Phoenix, Muskogee, Indian Territory, February 26, 1885.

Muskogee Phoenix, Muskogee, Indian Territory, February 24, 1887.

Muskogee Phoenix, Muskogee, Indian Territory, July 11, 1888.

Muskogee Phoenix, Muskogee, Indian Territory, February 24, 1898.

Muskogee Phoenix, Muskogee, Indian Territory, August 5, 1956.

New York Times, New York, New York, May 15, 1887.

New York Times, New York, New York, January 20, 1888.

Petersburg Daily Index-Appeal, Petersburg, Virginia, February 2, 1887.

Richmond Gazette, Richwood, Ohio, July 10, 1884.

Salina Journal, Salina, Kansas, June 8, 1952.

Statesville Daily Record, Statesville, North Carolina, January 18, 1972.

Territorial Topic, Purcell, Oklahoma, November 28, 1889.

Times-Democrat, Muskogee, Oklahoma, May 1, 1916.

Titusville Herald, Titusville, Pennsylvania, March 26, 1971.

Tulsa Daily Democrat, Tulsa, Oklahoma, September 28, 1885.

Tyrone Daily Herald, Tyrone, Pennsylvania, January 17, 1901.

Tyrone Daily Herald, Tyrone, Pennsylvania, November 17, 1901.

MAGAZINES

Burton, Art T. "Frontier Indian Police." *Oklahoma State Trooper Magazine,* Summer 1996.

Ernst, Robert. "Sam Sixkiller: Tragic Life of an Indian Lawman," *Frontier Times Magazine,* October 1984.

Foreman, Carolyn Thomas. "The Lighthorse in the Indian Territory." *Chronicles of Oklahoma,* Vol. 1 No. 34, January 1956.

Graebner, Norman A. "Public Land Policy of the Five Civilized Tribes." *Chronicles of Oklahoma,* VIX, June 1975.

Kappler, Charles J. *Indian Affairs: Laws and Treaties,* Vol. II. Washington: Government Printing Office.

Meserve, John B. "Chief Samuel Checote, with Sketches of Chiefs Locher Harjo and Ward Coachman." *Chronicles of Oklahoma,* Vol. 16 No. 4, December 1938.

Thomas, Robert B. *Farmer's Almanac.* Lewiston, ME: Almanac Publishing Company, 1878.

———. *Farmer's Almanac.* Lewiston, ME: Almanac Publishing Company, 1881.

———. *The Old Farmer's Almanac,* No. 91. Orange Co., NC: William Ware & Company, 1883.

Tuddenham, Susan. "After the Trail of Tears: The Cherokee in Oklahoma, 1838–1870." *The Concord Review, Inc.,* 1998.

Wayne T. Walker, "Captain Sixkiller–Indian Policeman" *Golden West Magazine,* Vol. 6 No. 1, November 1969.

Wright, Muriel H. "Early Navigation and Commerce Along the Arkansas and Red Rivers in Oklahoma," *Chronicles of Oklahoma,* VIII, March 1930.

WEBSITES

About Muskogee, www.cityofmuskogee.com.

Badman Dick Glass, www.rootsweb.ancestry.com.

Burton, Art T. "Black, Red and Deadly, Part II," Art Burton's Wild West, www.artburton.com.

Burton, Art T. "Oklahoma's Frontier Indian Police–Part 1." Art Burton's Wild West, www.artburton.com.

Burton, Art T. "Oklahoma' Frontier Indian Police–Part 2." Art Burton's Wild West, www.artburton.com.

Burton, Art T. "Oklahoma's Frontier Indian Police–Part 3." Art Burton's Wild West, www.artburton.com.

Chavez, Will. "Cherokee Historic Profiles." www.cherokeephoenix.org.

Cherokee Nation, www.cherokee.org, CHN II Vol. 270 and CHN 12 Vol. 275A.

Cherokee Nation, www.cherokee.org, CHN Vol. 270, 166.

Cherokee Nation, www.cherokee.org, CHN 12 Vol. 275A, 116.

Cherokee Removal, www.wikipedia.org.

The Dalton Gang, www.theoutlaws.com.

Dick Glass, www.digitallibrary.okstate.edu.

Early Muskogee, Oklahoma History, www.oklahomagenealogy.com.

Eddins, O. Ned. "Alcohol and the Indian Fur Trade," www.thefurtrapper.com.

Fort Gibson, www.wikipedia.org.

Freestone Past/Present, www.usgwarchives.net.

Indian Intercourse Act, www.wikipedia.org.

Introductory History of Denison, Texas, www.smalltownbigart.com.

Isaacs v. United States, 159 U.S. 487, www.supreme.justia.com.

Jay Gould Biography, www.biography.com; Jay Gould, www.wikipedia.com.

Legends of America, www.legendsofamerica.com.

Major Crimes Act, www.justice.gov.

Missouri-Kansas-Texas Railroad, www.wikipedia.org.

Missouri Pacific Railroad, www.katyrailroad.org.

Muskogee People, www.wikipedia.org.

Northrup, Brad. "Indians, Whites, and Alcohol." www.narhist.ewu.edu.

The Officer Down Memorial Page, Inc., www.odmp.org.

OK-Lawman-Outlaw-L Archives, www.listsearch.rootsweb.com.

Railroad History/KATY, www.oklahombres.org.

Sasakwa, Oklahoma, www.wikipedia.org.

Seminole Nation, www.seminolenation-indianterritory.org.

Shannon, J., Cherokee National Penitentiary, www.cityoftahlequah.com.

Tahlequah, Oklahoma, www.okstate.edu.

Tahlequah, Oklahoma, www.wikipedia.org.

Tahlequah City Directory, 1896, Indian Territory and Cherokee County, www.files.usgwarchives.net.

Trail of Tears, www.wikipedia.org.

Train Robberies, www.oklahombres.org.

22nd Generation, www.thecityobserver.org.

United States Indian Police, www.wikipedia.org.

United States v. Kagama, www.wikipedia.org.

Webber Falls, Oklahoma, www.wikipedia.org.

Wortham, Texas, www.wikipedia.org.

MANUSCRIPT MATERIAL

Annual Report of the Secretary of the Interior, Serv. 3915, 256.

Arrest Records for Alf Cunningham aka Ed Brown, United States Court System, Western District of Arkansas Records Department.

Arrest Records for Barney Sweeny, United States Court System, Western District of Arkansas Records Department.

Arrest Records for Charles Ashcroft, United States Court System, Western District of Arkansas Records Department.

Arrest Records for Dick Vann, United States Court System, Western District of Arkansas Records Department.

Arrest Records for Dick Vann and Alf Cunningham, United States Court System, Western District of Arkansas Records Department.

Arrest Records for Frank Bonds, United States Court System, Western District of Arkansas Records Department.

Arrest Records for Frank Woods, United States Court System, Western District of Arkansas Records Department.

Arrest Records for Henry Blake, United States Court System, Western District of Arkansas Records Department.

Arrest Records for Isaac Deer, United States Court System, Western District of Arkansas Records Department.

Arrest Records for Jeff Bollen, United States Court System, Western District of Arkansas Records Department.

Arrest Records for Milo Hoyt, United States Court System, Western District of Arkansas Records Department.

Arrest Records for Nathan Harris, United States Court System, Western District of Arkansas Records Department.

Arrest Records for One Franks, United States Court System, Western District of Arkansas Records Department.

Arrest Records for Solomon Coon, United States Court System, Western District of Arkansas Records Department.

Arrest Records for W. R. Fox, United States Court System, Western District of Arkansas Records Department.

Arrest Records for Willis Pettit, United States Court System, Western District of Arkansas Records Department.

Arrest Records for (First Name Unknown) Wright, United States Court System, Western District of Arkansas Records.

Bagby, Margaret Sixkiller Interview #T-559-3, University of Oklahoma, Western History Collection, Norman, Oklahoma.

Baggette, Pearl Interview #2122, University of Oklahoma, Western History Collection, Norman, Oklahoma.

Benson, D. F. Interview #7616, University of Oklahoma, Western History Collection, Norman, Oklahoma.

Congressional Recommendation, President James K. Polk, April 13, 1846.

Constitution of the Cherokee Nation, September 6, 1839.

Ferguson, Lu Interview #6990, University of Oklahoma, Western History Collection, Norman, Oklahoma.

Government Court Record, Eastern Band of Cherokee Indians vs. the U.S., March 1, 1886.

Government Report of Communion to Five Civilized Tribes, U.S. Interior Department, 138.

Hannon, John J. Interview #226, University of Oklahoma, Western History Collection, Norman, Oklahoma.

Hicks, H. W. Interview #7605, University of Oklahoma, Western History Collection, Norman, Oklahoma.

Lacey, Linda. "The White Man's Law and the American Indian Family in Assimilation Era." *Arkansas Law Review 40*, 1928.

Letter to Cherokee Agent Colonel J. McKisick from Chief George Lowrey, November 26, 1845.

Letter to Chief Perryman from Judge Isaac Parker, May 3, 1887, Creek Nation Relations File, University of Oklahoma, Western History Collection, Norman, Oklahoma.

Letter to Deputy US Marshal J. B. Jones from Chief Lewis Downing, Oklahoma Historical Society, Vol. 7, July 19, 1872.

Letter to Secretary of State James G. Blaine from Captain Sam Sixkiller, December 29, 1886.

Lewis, S. R. Interview #7699, University of Oklahoma, Western History Collection, Norman, Oklahoma.

Memories of Mrs. Dora Crittenden Pryor, DAR Section 1939–1942. Unpublished narratives of Oklahoma.

Records of the Indian Division, Office of the Secretary of the Interior, Special File 30-0864.

Redbird and Sam Sixkiller's Military Service Records, Reference #09011001, National Archives & Records Administration.

Sixkiller, Emma Interview, University of Oklahoma, Western History Collection, Norman, Oklahoma.

Sixkiller, Luke Interview #373, University of Oklahoma, Western History Collection, Norman, Oklahoma.

Sixkiller, Lynch Interview #64, University of Oklahoma, Western History Collection, Norman, Oklahoma.

Telegram from Captain Sam Sixkiller to Fort Smith Marshals, September 15, 1882.

United States Senate Document No. 120, 25th Congress.

Western History Collection, University of Oklahoma, Norman, Oklahoma, M452 Box 5 Folder 2.

Western History Collection, University of Oklahoma, Norman, Oklahoma, Bigby PS-149, April 19, 1937.

William, Justin, "Harsh Law for Indians," *North America Review,* March 1882.

AUTHOR INTERVIEWS AND CORRESPONDENCE

Baty, Charles (great-great-grandson of Sam Sixkiller). Correspondence with photos, July 7, 2011.

Baty, Charles (great-great-grandson of Sam Sixkiller). Telephone interview, July 12, 2010.

Index

ABOUT THE AUTHORS

Howard Kazanjian, an award-winning producer and entertainment executive, has been producing feature films and television programs for more than thirty years. While vice president of production for Lucasfilm Ltd., he produced two of the highest-grossing films of all time, *Raiders of the Lost Ark* and *Star Wars: Return of the Jedi.* Some of his other notable credits include *The Rookie, Demolition Man,* and the first season of *JAG.*

In addition to his production experience, Kazanjian has worked closely with some of the finest directors in the history of cinema, including Alfred Hitchcock, Billy Wilder, Sam Peckinpah, Robert Wise, Joshua Logan, Clint Eastwood, George Lucas, Steven Spielberg, Elia Kazan, and Francis Ford Coppola. He is a longtime voting member of the Academy of Motion Picture Arts and Sciences, the Academy of Television Arts and Sciences, the Producers Guild of America, and the Directors Guild of America.

Chris Enss has been writing about women of the Old West for more than ten years. She loves Western culture and travels quite extensively, collecting research for her books. She received the Spirit of the West Alive award, cosponsored by the *Wild West Gazette,* celebrating her efforts to keep the spirit of the Old West alive for future generations. She currently lives in a historic gold-mining town in Northern California.